Like
Some Green Laurel

Library of Southern Civilization

Lewis P. Simpson, Editor

Like
Some Green Laurel

Letters of

Margaret Johnson Erwin

1821–1863

JOHN SEYMOUR ERWIN

Louisiana State University Press / Baton Rouge and London

Designer: Albert Crochet
Typeface: VIP Goudy Old Style
Typesetter: LSU Press
Printer and binder: Thomson-Shore, Inc.

LIBRARY OF CONGRESS CATALOGING IN PUBLICATION DATA
Erwin, Margaret Johnson 1821–1863.
  Like some green laurel.

  (Library of Southern civilization)
  Bibliography: p.
  Includes index.
  1. Erwin, Margaret Johnson, 1821–1863. 2. United
States—Biography. I. Erwin, John Seymour, 1911– II. Title.
CT275.E715A4   973.6'0924 [B]   80-23545
ISBN 0-8071-0761-1

May she become a flourishing hidden tree
That all her thoughts may like the linnet be,
And have no business but dispensing round
Their magnanimities of sound,
Nor but in merriment begin a chase,
Nor but in merriment a quarrel.
O may she live like some green laurel
Rooted in one dear perpetual place.

from "A Prayer for My Daughter," W. B. Yeats

Contents

List of Illustrations

Mrs. Junius R. Ward (née Matilda Viley)
Elizabeth Ward McGehee
William Tecumseh Sherman
John Cabell Breckinridge

Preface

In the summer of 1937 I was introduced belatedly to my great-grandmother through some of her letters which were then in the possession of Mr. A. S. W. Rosenbach of Philadelphia. At an informal gathering in that city, Mr. Rosenbach told me that he had a collection of documents from a Margaret Johnson Erwin of Kentucky and Mississippi. Most of the letters were written to the Philadelphia architect Samuel Sloan. Mr. Rosenbach was amused by the coincidence of names, and that I should come from Mississippi—from the same locale, too.

I was struck by the dates of the letters, which were contemporary with my great-grandmother and I soon determined that she and the letter writer were indeed the same. Most surprising was to hear her name at a party in Philadelphia, for she had long been an almost legendary figure to me; her family-remembered capers, feuds, outspokenness, and adamant character were—locally—legendary.

The letters in the possession of Mr. Rosenbach were loosely placed in cardboard boxes; they were not filed and were in no order. At each session with them I had some hours to examine, read, take notes, or dismiss those that did not appeal to me. Being quite young, I looked only for what seemed an amusing or outrageous opinion. Too, the sudden appearance of a familiar or famous name served as a guide for what then interested me, with no thought as to whether it was of importance or concern to anyone else.

It must be remembered that I attached no value to the letters beyond the fact that they were titillating and I felt some faint pride in their having a personal relationship to me. In discussions of this with Mr. Rosenbach he said that I might have them or use them in any way that I saw fit. But once again a youthful carelessness took over; and although I took my notebooks away with me when I tired of my copying chore, I did not want to be bothered with two awkward boxes of assorted and faded papers.

My great mistake lay in not accepting the offer of copying the correspondence *in toto* or carting it away, as suggested by Mr. Rosenbach. I had no intention then of ever using the letters. At the time I transcribed a few outstanding (Margaret Erwin would have called them "outlandish") views and opinions and showed them to several people, among them William Alexander Percy and Maxwell Perkins. Both were briefly immobilized with laughter.

Not long after, I entered the Royal Canadian Air Force as a volunteer and my papers along with other possessions were put into storage. There they remained for over four years. When the war was over and I returned to New York, the notebooks were unpacked and shoved into file drawers, untranscribed and —again—forgotten.

Early in the 1960s, while looking for some misplaced item, I came across the books and opened one. Transcribing my own cryptic brand of shorthand at this late point was like trying to learn a long forgotten language in Cyrillic. But what I labored through in the first half hour so stirred my interest that over the next few months I continued to read and set down in longhand what exists today. After typing a few pages I showed these efforts to a friend or two, one of them an editor. It was through this casual beginning that the idea formed of transcribing all the bits and pieces that I had copied so many years earlier. Then I tried putting them into some sort of chronological order and took stock. The results still did not seem to make much sense and my efforts seemed wasted. At the same time I was nagged on by some vague interest; as this grew Margaret Erwin's letters began to take the form that they are in today.

But in the process there were some deadly weeks and months between. For beyond the transcribing of the correspondence came the job of putting events mentioned into their correct niches in history. Many letters were not dated (or in my carelessness I had not seen fit to include the date) and too many existed as fragments without a beginning and without an end.

Because of several genealogy maniacs in my family I had long been turned away from the subject except for some few awesome highlights. How much I agree with what would have been Margaret Erwin's attitude toward the use of the word *roots* when not applied to a tree or rosebush! Yet I was drawn into examining the puzzle of Margaret Johnson Erwin and there was no escape. I cannot say that I have many of the answers and I feel that no one else has or will ever have.

From notes taken from many sources throughout recent years, I have assembled in as near to chronological order as possible the story of the building of Mount Holly, of its brief day, and of its owner and her prophetic views on the nation's immediate (and its continuing) follies and agonies.

Of particular interest to me were the notes regarding the contemporary personalities who passed across Margaret Johnson Erwin's stage, both the full-blown characters and the shadow figures. Another facet of interest is the unusual amount of travel that this atypical woman of the mid-nineteenth century accomplished in adventures that ranged from taking tea at Windsor Castle with Queen Victoria to falling off a donkey on her way to stir up the oracle at Delphi. Her language was colorful, her opinions intractable, and her humor unlimited (and, more often than not, directed at herself).

Margaret Erwin's life, while appallingly short, was a forty-three year tragicomedy. *She* knew it, and for the most part enjoyed every moment of it. Mount Holly was the scene of a procession of other characters whose names stand out in American political and cultural life and history. The visitors, guests or friends (and she made the distinction) whom she entertained included Louis Moreau Gottschalk, Generals Albert Sidney Johnston and J. C. Pemberton, John J. Audubon's two sons, George Caleb Bingham, John Pope, and Stephen A. Douglas (an old friend of her brother Matthew), who, she said, "always seems to show up at Matt's when Mr. Lincoln has displeased him!"

In addition to many of the talented, literate, and renowned persons of her day, there came into Margaret's association those figures whose shadowy politics or military positions required a certain amount of diplomacy in her relations with them, an art for which she had great ability and equally great distaste. Nevertheless Margaret's broad and at some times radical opinions alienated much of the family. Soon after her marriage to James Erwin, "words" with her brother Matthew led to a coolness, then estrangement, which lasted all their later years. Relations with her father seem to have become closer and closer to outright hostility as the war approached, and by the time of the war she was cut off from close kin and cousins as well as friends who found it difficult to come to grips with the political morass at hand. Meanwhile, Margaret freed her slaves in 1858. Her prophetic pronouncements preceded the national conflict by some fifteen years; even today we are dealing with some of her precognitions.

But in this forthright and outspoken nature she was not alone in the family. Her favorite uncle was Richard Mentor Johnson, vice president under Van Buren. Margaret was possibly the only member of the Johnson clan who condoned his "romance" (her word) and subsequent marriage to his octoroon mistress, Julia Chinn. She sat back and watched close and distant kin shudder or become stiff-lipped; she wrote that she thought she would "choke with laughter at the effect of the name on Matt and the others." Margaret Johnson Erwin liked opinions. Had Lucifer appeared with his cohorts I am sure she would have put them up for a night or so just to hear their side of the Fall.

In another vein, these letters that we have attest to a long friendship that sustained Margaret, and in these we see a side of her that is as sympathetic and deep-feeling as her tongue is sharp. Until midway in my research the woman named "Carrie" remained an annoying puzzle. Her exact relationship to Margaret Erwin and to the Sloan family in Philadelphia remains in the shadow, but at last I discovered her full name was Caroline Wilson. As the letters reveal, Carrie was a friend of long standing and she made several trips to England and the Continent with Margaret.

Mount Holly exists today as a sort of monument to a highly energetic, irrepressible woman, amazingly well educated and traveled for her day—and to a great architect, Samuel Sloan. Sloan was a pupil of William Strickland who, in turn, was a student of Latrobe, an architect of the City of Washington. He is probably best known in the South for the Moorish palace, Longwood, that he began for Dr. Haller Nutt in Natchez. Strickland's work dots the southern and eastern landscape, from Rattle and Snap in Nashville to the Philadelphia Exchange building.

Mount Holly, for all its strange touches, is primarily Italianate in design. It does not differ in too many ways from other houses of the period, which were for the most part Strawberry Hill Gothic or late offshoots of the declining Greek Revival or early San Francisco Wedding Cake. Yet the house *is* different—it does lack symmetry and it has innovations not seen in many homes of its day: among them are an extraordinary amount of plumbing, a gas-light system, and several dining rooms. At times, the efforts to achieve these feats carried the Erwin-Sloan friendship to the edge of a precipice, always of Margaret Erwin's making. Along with the letters found in the Rosenbach collection were sketches she had made—"suggestions," she called them. Her changes of mind, from letter to letter, were enough to make any architect want to end it all by leaping from his drafting board. In the collection, too, were some of the original drawings, elevations, and estimates.

Margaret Erwin was a woman who knew what she wanted, and it was a rare day that she did not get it. When that day came, however, the fate of the South as she knew it had been decided. The house itself was never at any stage more complete than it can be seen today: some balustrades remain in wood that were to have been iron; niches in the entrance hall are still bare of the sculpture ordered to fill them. The marble mantels and statuary for the hall, which were to come from Italy, probably lie in some fathoms of water off the Atlantic or Gulf Coast. But this is understandable, for in 1861 all work came to a halt and many items of decoration or furnishing were lost or halted in the blockade. The house is a palatable cake but the icing is missing. Samuel Sloan's southern "masterpiece"—Longwood, in Natchez—suffered even more severely than Mount Holly, in that only one floor out of six was finished.

Although the house was essentially complete by 1859, Margaret Erwin did not live even half a decade to enjoy it. By the time of her death in 1863 she had seen her first husband die and a favorite stepson (Andrew Eugene Erwin) killed in the Civil War. Several others of her children and many members of her family had also died. The last year of her life found her a somewhat lost and lonely woman. At her death, the only members of her family present were a son, Johnson Erwin, some of the

Ward family, Charles Dudley, Margaret's second husband, and their son, Charles, Jr.

Eleven years prior to her death she had been surrounded by three of the five of James Erwin's children by his first wife, Anne Clay (some with their families), and their own five offspring. After she was gone, Johnson Erwin sold "80 percent of his interest in Mount Holly to the Dudleys, father and son (in 1880)." The Erwins then moved to Junius Ward's temporary "summer house" (then called Fair Oaks, now Erwin). The elder Wards, Mr. and Mrs. Junius, Sr., died at Erwin after witnessing the loss of Ward Hall and most of their wealth, in Kentucky. In 1855–56, they had seen an amplified but uncompleted duplication of their Kentucky house—a large Greek Revival structure with Palladian overtones—swallowed by the Mississippi at Princeton (or Washington) Landing, near Kentucky Bend.

The Charles Dudleys, Sr. and Jr., did not live long after the Erwin move from Mount Holly and after their deaths the house and plantation passed to the Colwell family of Memphis. They held it but briefly. Around 1898, Mr. and Mrs. Huger Foote, Sr., lived there for about a decade. When they gave it up it was bought by Dr. and Mrs. Albert Lee and it remained in their hands until Mrs. Lee's death in 1956. The John Coxes owned Mount Holly until 1979 when it passed to the C. W. Wood family, who are in the midst of restoring the house and grounds.

I was fortunate enough to live through twenty-five years of my grandmother's reign; she was Matilda Ward, Margaret Erwin's daughter-in-law. From her I got much firsthand information of the earliest part of Mount Holly's existence. I spent two boyhood years at Monteagle, Tennessee, in the same house with Mrs. Foote, Sr., and have her accounts of later days of the house and plantation, in the first decade of this century.

The continuing history of Mount Holly is a combination of local gossip and hearsay. Following Margaret Erwin's death her daughter Lillie (then Mrs. Oliver Morgan) returned to the plantation frequently to take charge of the other children. When it was impossible for her to do so Margaret's sisters, Emily or Louisa, came to look after the badly shaken household. It seems that Johnson Erwin, my grandfather, was the most lost of the family; at age thirteen he became dependent on and devoted to his sister, Lillie, and his aunts "Em" and "Lou."

He had little in common with his half brother, Charles Dudley, Jr., and became a regular visitor at the Junius Wards' next door. From this frequent association grew his attachment to the youngest and somewhat spoiled daughter of that family, Matilda, whom he eventually married in 1874. I know little of Victor Flournoy and William beyond their birth and death dates; William went to Washington, dying there in 1908. Victor lived on the lake and died in the 1880s during one of the sporadic outbreaks of yellow fever, and lies buried in the orchard at Erwin.

From all accounts while life at Mount Holly may have been sobered by Margaret's death it did not end. Even with the South's economic difficulties following the war Margaret's house once again became the scene of house parties, regattas on the lake, and hunting parties there and at nearby Swan Lake. Old friends from the North and East began to appear once more. Margaret's sister Emily had lost her husband and a few years after Margaret's death she married the widowed Dr. Dudley. By the time Johnson Erwin and Matilda Ward were married a few years later social activity was booming. Among the guests from the North was Marshall Field, who was a member of the Swan Lake Gun Club. An incident that smoldered for many years was the cause of my grandmother's indignation when he asked one evening at dinner what she would ask for an enormous Sevres dinner service. "Mattie" never spoke to, or of, him again.

Dr. Dudley and his sister-in-law/ wife continued to entertain large gatherings of Johnsons, Worthingtons, Erwins and others—with Matt Johnson in the spotlight, much to the displeasure of Margaret's spirit, no doubt. Then Dr. Dudley died and his widow left the lake and went to live in Pennsylvania.

Young Charles Dudley kept up the activities of Mount Holly, gradually amplifying them to where scandalous episodes were more to be expected than not. Alcohol, wild gambling, and strange characters became synonymous with his name. Then on one summer evening Charlie died of "overindulgence" at a dinner party at neighboring New Hope Plantation. On his death it was found that he had badly depleted all the resources of the plantation. In one way it was fortunate that Johnson, Victor, William, and the girls had sold out to him the year of his death, but it was ironic that Johnson and Matilda Erwin had moved from Mount Holly to Erwin only a month or six weeks before. For had they remained that short length of time it becomes a bitter bit of retrospect that the house would probably have remained in the family.

Acknowledgments

The descendants of the Johnson family have been of great assistance in my efforts to put this chronicle together: special thanks to the late Mrs. Morgan Johnson of Greenville, Mississippi, and members of the Kansas, Kentucky, New York, New Mexico, and Virginia branches.

Perhaps the first germ of an idea for some practical use of the letters came from William Alexander Percy, the late lawyer, planter, poet, and author of the autobiographical *Lanterns on the Levee*. After reading five or six excerpts, he laughed and quoted her, "Quite a woman—'afraid most of the real characters have gone. Those that are left are mentally attenuated, or worse.'"

I am indebted to the late Willa Johnson of Greenville, Mississippi, for documents and for information regarding the history of the Johnsons in both Kentucky and Mississippi. "Willie," as she was known to her family and most of her friends, was literate, provocative and an irascible character; according to any perceptive viewer, and to the noted photographers Arnold Genthe and Clarence White, she was a great photographer, one of the best of her day. Some of the historical research for the WPA Mississippi State Guide was done by her; what appears in the printed volume is correct in each detail. However,

Acknowledgments

other documents connected with her and quoted here must be viewed in the unfortunate light of bias and the bottle. Willie was often carried away by both. In addition to her remarkable qualities, she was by turns voluble and terse; she was a firm holder of opinions, an inveterate gambler, and either a delight or a devil to those who knew her.

I owe much in particular to Mr. Clinton Ikerd Bagley of the Mississippi State Department of Archives and History. His research could not have been more intelligently directed or thorough.

Among the many who have contributed material knowledge and authenticated documents, insights as to the historical worth of Mount Holly, and specific advice along the way, I express my gratitude to: Mrs. Paula M. Alexander, Mrs. Jessie Lucretia Erwin Anderson, Mrs. Julia Ward Blanchard, the late Wallace Brockway, Miss Marguerie Burnham, Colonel Robert P. Clay, Professor Harold N. Cooledge, Jr., Mr. and Mrs. John Cox, Mrs. Hal DeCell, Miss Olivia de Havilland, Mr. and Mrs. David Dewey, the late Mr. Drew Dudley, Mr. Michael Ellison, the late Mrs. Junius Ward Erwin, the late Mrs. Matilda Ward Erwin, Mr. Thomas Erwin, Mrs. Victor Flournoy Erwin, the Reverend James Harold Flye, the late Mrs. Huger Foote, Sr., the late Mr. Ford Madox Ford, Mr. and Mrs. Walter Fox, Mr. Stewart R. James, Mr. and Mrs. Frank Jennings.

Also, Mrs. Morgan Johnson, Mr. Bern Keating, Mr. Carlyle Klise, Mr. Seymour Kurtz, Mr. Clay Lancaster, Mr. Gerstle Mack, Miss Dawn Maddox, Mrs. Margaret S. Mallett, Miss Roberta Miller, Mr. Carl McIntire, Miss Frances Percy McNeily, Mr. Murray Miller, Mrs. Sara Farish Percy, the late Mr. William Alexander Percy, the late Mr. Maxwell Perkins, the late Mrs. Isabelle Ward Pollard, Miss Carolyn Pollard, Mr. Robert S. Reynolds, Mr. James Saylor, Mrs. Margaret Erwin Shutt and Mr. William John Shutt, Jr., Mr. Harvey Simmonds, Mrs. Cyn-

Acknowledgments

thia Stone, Mr. and Mrs. Charles Verral, Mrs. Helene Jordan Waddell, Mrs. Angela Woods and Mrs. Frances H. Wright. In the preparation of *Like Some Green Laurel* special credit must go to Robert S. Reynolds of New York City. He has steadily assisted me throughout the years while these letters were being correlated and the transitional material was being written and researched, and he has checked and prepared drafts of the manuscript time and again until the final one was considered ready to go to the publishers. And, during all stages of readying the book, he has continued to make especially helpful editorial suggestions. Now that all is folded and filed and the project is, for my part, creatively at an end, I want to acknowledge that, in a very real sense, its moving from rough idea to finished product owes more than I can say to his support, enthusiasm, and taste.

Also I would like to express gratitude to Dr. Mary Ann Payne for personal reasons too numerous to mention. My appreciation to the LSU Press staff for their patience and care in producing this book, and my special thanks to Marie Blanchard, whose suggestions and counsel were invaluable, and who gathered together the many loose threads, making of them whole cloth.

PART I

The Early Years

I wailed long and loudly when I was forcibly removed by Mammy Sam from the dignified old gentleman's knee. It remains remarkable to me how a child's memory may hold one small event, a first memory of any one thing. I must have been between the ages of four and five; I should have been caned and sent packing. But I wasn't and the reason for my evident and audible displeasure when taken away was because the gentleman smelled so good.

Margaret Johnson Erwin wrote this to her friend Carrie Wilson describing her brief encounter with the Marquis de Lafayette. He was visiting her Uncle Richard (Richard Mentor Johnson) at Blue Springs, his Kentucky plantation home. Henry Clay was present and "twitted me long after I was grown about my violent behavior."

Clay visited Johnson with the French general and together they went back to Ashland, Clay's home in Lexington (1825). This was one of Lafayette's last visits to the United States. In and around the towns of Versailles, Paris, Frankfort, Georgetown, and Lexington, the marquis evidently found a sense of kinship with the Kentuckians who had settled in the Bluegrass country.

By the time of this visit, the whole of the Mississippi Valley region was dotted with French settlements—east to Kentucky and west to St. Louis and down the river to New Orleans. Some of these dated from the time that French Louisiana stretched from the Gulf of Mexico northward and westward to the Rockies and to Spain's possessions in the southwest. Many families were refugees from the Terror in France, and it is more than legend that among those who fled, like the aristocratic Huguenot Flournoys, are those who came to the young United States to prepare a place of exile for Louis XVI and Marie Antoinette and their children.

Under the influence of their mother Elizabeth Flournoy, Margaret Johnson and some of her sisters and brothers and their close friends spoke French as fluently as they spoke English. We see something of her love for languages and learning in this comment about her brother: "Matt makes such sport of us—but Matt is an oaf. He thinks my Latin and Greek and Italian are just to assuage my vanity. What an utter fool!"

These Kentuckians of the early to mid-nineteenth century were a gay and carefree people, riding the highest wave they were ever to know. The small settlements that had begun in the 1700s—with Louisville as their center—had become self-assured and sometimes truculent, and could shake their bustles in the faces of their arrogant and often less genteel sisters. There was a time, even, when Lexington, then Louisville, were considered the logical center for the capital of the nation.

A major step in Louisville's progress came with the arrival of the steamboat *New Orleans*, which stopped there on its maiden voyage south from Pittsburgh in 1811. This marked the beginning of the steamboat era. In 1815 the incomparable *Enterprise* scurried up the river from New Orleans to Louisville in twelve days. Prosperity was just around the bend and was not long in making itself seen and heard.

The Partland Canal was opened in 1830 to the Falls of the Ohio and the river's narrow channel. It was then that Louisville came into its own as an important halfway stop for river

4

commerce between Pittsburgh and New Orleans. Later, St. Louis and Memphis would have their share of trade and traffic —but Louisville stepped in first, tripping all contenders.

In the 1830s, Louisville boasted two excellent hotels, famous even to this day: the Galt House and the Louisville. The latter became a criterion for hotels in the south and midwest. The Galt House was razed in 1920, a victim of that too common lack of concern and tradition which underlies the frequent failure of Americans to preserve anything of artistic or historical worth. Among its admiring guests had been Charles Dickens and Lafayette, both of whom compared it favorably with anything they had patronized in Paris.

Well into this century it continued to be clear that the city, like most American cities, had by 1850 realized that England's Victoria reigned over all as architectural spirit. Soaring, lace-trimmed monstrosities were augmented a little later by the social aspirations of the *nouveaux riches* with their chateaux and manor houses.

Louisville's original population came from the Carolinas, Virginia, and Maryland; then came the New Englanders who, for the most part, felt the local culture inferior to their own. Yet, with their tidy accounting-book minds and much anticipatory hand rubbing, they came anyway, to bask in the affluence and material possibilities of the new frontier. When it came to a confrontation and inevitable division of political minds, particularly when the "war between the states" began, most of them hot-footed it back to the comparative security of Beacon Hill. When the first wave of emancipation was under way and the first settlement had grown into villages and towns, the Kentuckians retained the sense of their past.

The French émigrés had a great impact on Louisville, culturally and financially. Although many could carry little of material worth from France because of the revolution, they brought industry and skills to the (then) western city. Audubon came

5

with his vast knowledge of botany and other natural sciences and his great skills in painting; Tarazon saw the possibilities of the powerful and noisy Falls and utilized them for industry; music was brought to the city by the duc d'Orleans, later Louis Philippe, king of France; manufacturing was introduced by J. Barbaroux and shipping was given impetus through the efforts and talents of Ed. Honoré, Henri Berthoud, and Pierre Tardiveau. The acceptance of these French refugees by the American pioneers is still remembered by the faint traces of a certain Gallic culture existing to an appreciable extent now only in mid-Kentucky and in New Orleans.

The 1840s brought disaster. A fire destroyed much of the city, but Louisville was rebuilt and its growth was unabated. In addition to its large French and English population, Germans began arriving in great numbers. They added little that was tangible and of industrial worth, but the culture they possessed became an integral part of what Louisville would eventually become.

By 1850, the population was almost 45,000. From then on it became a picture of America in midstream—its politics were rambunctious and, regrettably, often crooked; its civil law at times was even more so. Its culture, however, occasionally dimmed that of New York and the whole east. Louisville had "firsts" in concerts, in exhibitions and innovations in the medical and other sciences that predated eastern achievements by years.

Louisville's musical history alone offers quite a few surprises. It and Lexington had many premier performances, both native and foreign. It is startling to read that Beethoven's First Symphony got one of its initial U.S. hearings in a Kentucky metropolis. [1] The reason is still a matter of mulling, for conjecture, for reflecting. Perhaps it was the invasion of European cultures that,

1. H. Earle Johnson, *First Performances in America* (Detroit: College Music Society), 35.

finding no really open-armed welcome elsewhere on this continent, were naturally drawn to a people who still retained the amenities of their homelands and by whom they were easily and unquestionably accepted. Or perhaps it was Louisville's effort to go one measured and leisurely step beyond its competitors. Whatever it was, it succeeded. At times New York, Boston, Philadelphia—and certainly Washington—smoldered. Only New Orleans could look Louisville in the eye and wink. In viewing each other, they offered a unique and affectionate mutual respect.

Among the early pioneers of the Ohio Valley was the Ward family. Of the original Ward settlers, Stephen was probably a "straight-shooting," honorable man. As for his brother William, there are some speculations about his eye-to-eye honesty. General William Ward repudiated Simon Kenton's joint claim to the land on which most of Urbana (Ohio) now stands, and it was he and his sons, Junius and Robert, who profited by it—and who later lost it all.

By the time their cousin Margaret Johnson was born, Louisville had become the home of Robert Ward. His brother Junius had acquired much property near Lexington, between Frankfort and Georgetown, and seems to have been the more stable member of the family. He married a homely, well-educated girl, Matilda Viley. Robert married Emily Flournoy, sister of Elizabeth Flournoy (who was Margaret Johnson's mother).

Robert Ward was soon known as one of the wealthiest members of the community, with a social standing *assoluta*, but was also known locally and nationally for his gambling. This took the form of horse racing, cards, and wild wagering upon anything that stood still or moved and on which money could be won or lost. He dabbled in the arts, considering himself something of a connoisseur; he sponsored some of George Caleb Bingham's early work and bought *The County Election*. He aided in

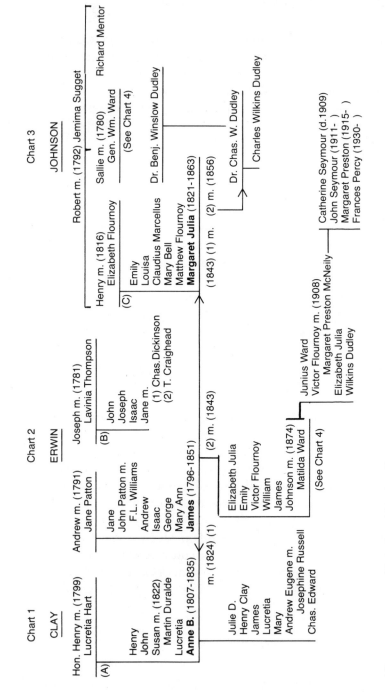

Chart 1

Chart 2

Chart 3

CLAY

ERWIN

JOHNSON

Hon. Henry m. (1799)
Lucretia Hart

Andrew m. (1791)
Jane Patton

Joseph m. (1781)
Lavinia Thompson

Robert m. (1792) Jemima Sugget

Henry m. (1816)
Elizabeth Flournoy

Sallie m. (1780)
Gen. Wm. Ward

Richard Mentor

(A)

Henry
John
Susan m. (1822)
Martin Duralde
Lucretia
Anne B. (1807-1835)

Jane
John Patton m.
F.L. Williams
Andrew
Isaac
George
Mary Ann
James (1796-1851)

(B)

John
Joseph
Isaac
Jane m.
(1) Chas. Dickinson
(2) T. Craighead

(C)

Emily
Louisa
Claudius Marcellus
Mary Bell
Matthew Flournoy
Margaret Julia (1821-1863)

(See Chart 4)

Dr. Benj. Winslow Dudley

(1843) (1) m.   (2) m. (1856)

Dr. Chas. W. Dudley

Charles Wilkins Dudley

m. (1824) (1)

(2) m. (1843)

Julie D.
Henry Clay
James
Lucretia
Mary
Andrew Eugene m.
Josephine Russell
Chas. Edward

Elizabeth Julia
Emily
Victor Flournoy
William
James
Johnson m. (1874)
Matilda Ward

(See Chart 4)

Junius Ward
Victor Flournoy m. (1908)
Margaret Preston McNeily
Elizabeth Julia
Wilkins Dudley

Catherine Seymour (d.1909)
John Seymour (1911-)
Margaret Preston (1915-)
Frances Percy (1930-)

(A) 6 other children   (B) 4 other children   (C) 5 other children

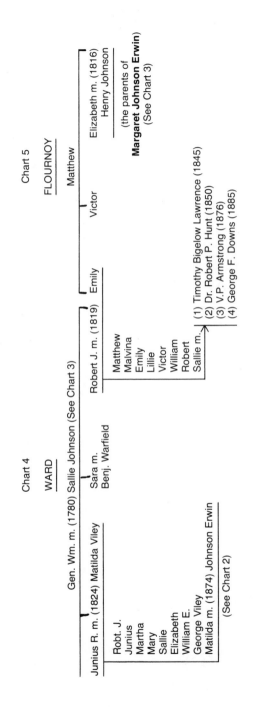

Chart 4

Chart 5

WARD

FLOURNOY

Gen. Wm. m. (1780) Sallie Johnson (See Chart 3)

Matthew

Junius R. m. (1824) Matilda Viley

Sara m.
Benj. Warfield

Robert J. m. (1819)

Emily

Victor

Elizabeth m. (1816)
Henry Johnson

(the parents of
Margaret Johnson Erwin)
(See Chart 3)

Robt. J.
Junius
Martha
Mary
Sallie
Elizabeth
William E.
George Viley
Matilda m. (1874) Johnson Erwin

(See Chart 2)

Matthew
Malvina
Emily
Lillie
Victor
William
Robert
Sallie m.

(1) Timothy Bigelow Lawrence (1845)
(2) Dr. Robert P. Hunt (1850)
(3) V.P. Armstrong (1876)
(4) George F. Downs (1885)

Family charts of Margaret Johnson and James Erwin

having engravings made of this well-known painting, both as gifts for his friends and for sale to the public.[2] Others who profited from his spending were the young Audubon brothers; their father, John J., had painted a number of the family's portraits, as had John Pope and George P. A. Healey.

The extravagances of Margaret's Louisville aunt and uncle, the Robert Wards, were phenomenal. It was a large family, with one exceptional daughter, a flamboyant belle named Sallie. From all accounts (including her portrait by George P. A. Healey and a miniature in *Famous Belles of the Nineteenth Century* by Virginia Peacock), Sallie Ward was an "astonishingly pretty [not beautiful] girl, brown haired, blue eyed, gay, unconventional, spoiled, and high-handed. But withal she was generous, amiable, and possessed an infallible ability to enchant and please."

While in her teens, Sallie traveled abroad, dined with the French emperor, was generally daring in her behavior; and her dress for most of her life bordered on the fantastic. Having become a disciple of Amelia Bloomer, she once stunned proper Bostonians into speechlessness by appearing in Turkish trousers, a turban, and jeweled sandals. When elegant occasions demanded the most of her, she always wore fresh roses in her hair—with real diamonds glued to the petals to resemble dew drops.

Margaret Johnson was twenty-seven when Sallie was married in Louisville, and acted as matron-of-honor at her wedding. For the rest of her life she watched her cousin Sallie out of the corner of her eye. She did not approve of Sallie's carelessness and preoccupation with every known vanity and frivolity, but no one could help but be amused. And Margaret's appreciation of

2. In the light of changing views, times, and places it may be of interest to know that Robert Ward bought *The County Election* for $1,000. Later in the nineteenth century it sold for $15,000 and is now in the St. Louis Mercantile Library. Another, lesser known Bingham painting, *The Jolly Flatboatmen* (one of several by that name) sold, in 1978, for $980,000.

the humor in the situations sometimes shows through. When someone rides a horse up the steps of the Galt House, into the lobby, then dashes away through the outdoor marketplace, scattering chickens, humans, and apples with no apparent concern for any of them, what can one say? Sallie Ward—up to her usual behavior.

Sallie, returning from Europe in her late teens, met one Timothy Bigelow Lawrence, the son of Abbott Lawrence, United States minister to Great Britain (1849–1852). They were from Boston and according to reports of the time, they were a family that might have entered into John Bossidy's toast of 1910 (based on an earlier 1880 version):

> And this is good old Boston,
> The home of the bean and the cod
> Where the Lowells talk to the Cabots
> And the Cabots talk only to God.

It was suspected that the Lawrences, too, only deigned to speak to the Almighty.

Timothy B. Lawrence, it is reported, was a handsome man. But he was remote and frigid; Sallie undertook to thaw him, and their engagement was announced soon after. Margaret Johnson, as a member of the wedding party, must have left a play-by-play description, right up to the final bell with the victor's hand in the air, but this has not survived.

Three husbands followed Sallie's divorce—a word not acceptable in polite society of the time—which had been preceded by some rather scandalous allegations (on the part of both Sallie and Timothy). The Lawrence divorce was accomplished only through the action of the Massachusetts legislature. Sallie's next two husbands conveniently died: Dr. Robert Hunt and V. P. Armstrong. She lived on in Louisville's Galt House, in diminishing elegance but with unassailable social position, until her death in 1896. Her fourth husband, George Downs, survived her. Sallie's funeral took place on the day that William Jennings Bryan delivered his famous "Cross of Gold" speech, bemoaning the "toiling masses" and "the brow of Labor." This Sallie would have promptly delivered to the fire on the hearth or the waste basket.

In contrast to Sallie Ward, Margaret Johnson took her privileged position as a right, yes, but also as a responsibility. In her we witness the character of the aristocrat, wherein learning and refinement set one apart for a purpose: those at the head of the society must take the lead. Though Margaret's role in life was as a matron and a mother, she held an avid interest in national politics and harkened back to the republican values that were the basis of the nation. As the Civil War approached, she found proof of her opinion that the country was being led to destruction by men of less than noble dimensions. Meanwhile, it was her endeavor to keep her mind alert and to provide for her spirit through exposure to the best of people and of art, especially music, as well as providing beautiful surroundings for herself and her family.

From the beginning, Margaret was adventuresome and active. Some years before Sallie Ward's first marriage, Margaret Johnson met Caroline Wilson, who became her lifelong friend. They were both twenty years of age. Margaret and Carrie had set off for Europe with "dowdy and prim Miss Beam" as chaperone. Poor Miss Beam. She barely survived the voyage to England and was prostrate the whole time.

The two girls were left on their own by a distant cousin of the Johnsons [or Flournoys?], Lady Lyttleton, who was supposed to keep an eye on them. Lady Lyttleton, trapped and rendered distraught by official duties in the royal household, apparently let the girls do pretty much as they pleased—and their own way they went, indeed.

They were helped by Lady Lyttleton's daughter, Lady A[lice?], "not exactly a spinster without ideas of her own," Margaret

10

wrote. Despite the problems of nineteenth century travel, they saw much of England in five weeks. Margaret was deeply immersed in English history—in fact, in world history. Yet she thought the Tower of London one of "the dreariest piles of stone" she had ever "*had* to be polite about." She went to the theater and opera constantly and viewed the city from end to end; through the good services of Lady Lyttleton, she and Carrie saw much that was not then open to the public.

PART II

1843–1851

James Erwin was one of six sons born to Andrew Erwin and Jane Patton, both from Tennessee and Kentucky by way of the Carolinas. The Erwin ancestry went back to Aberdeenshire in Scotland. The recorded line began when William de Irvine became armor bearer to Robert the Bruce, who presented Irvine with the Tower of Drum (February 13, 1323). It stands today still inhabited by the family.

A few hundred years after that event, several of the Erwin brothers left Bristol, England, for the colonies, settling first in Virginia, then moving southward and westward. As the family increased, Andrew Erwin and his wife, Jane, left the Carolinas for Tennessee, accompanied by his brother Joseph, Joseph's wife Lavinia Thompson, her parents, and several children. They acquired much property around Nashville and in eastern Tennessee. From their great plantation, Peach Blossom, they went to Louisiana, where they purchased substantial tracts of land. At one time they owned eleven or twelve plantations, including Shady Grove, St. Louis (or Home) and Evergreen.

The migrating Erwins made names for themselves in law, publishing, and as planters, but the Carolina-based Erwins, of all the family, seemed destined to be the ones to prosper—from

Alexander Erwin as founder of the Erwin Cotton Mills of South Carolina up to this century's Senator Sam Ervin.

It was mainly during this period of the dividing and settling in different locations that the spelling of the name began to vary, with even brothers differing the spelling from an *I* or an *E*. In some cases an *e* was added at the end of the name (possibly due to some clerk's flair for florid writing). The name began to mutate: Irving, Irwin, Erwin, Erwine. The "de" was lopped off late in the fourteenth century.

The Pattons, Scots-Irish, settled in Virginia and then spread out through several states, including the Carolinas and Kentucky. It was in the Carolinas that Jane Patton became the wife of Andrew Erwin. Her elder brother was the ancestor of General George S. Patton, of the Civil War, and of his namesake, famous in World War II.

James was born in Asheville, North Carolina, in 1796. Later the Andrew Erwins settled in Lexington, Kentucky; Joseph and Lavinia Erwin in Nashville, Tennessee. In Kentucky, James ingratiated himself with the Henry Clay household at Ashland and soon became a protégé of Clay himself, who eventually took him into his law office. To cap matters, James kept the trails between Tennessee and Kentucky warm with his frequent trips to Lexington in pursuit of Clay's daughter, Anne Brown. This culminated in their marriage in 1823, in Cahaba, Alabama, where Anne was visiting friends and where James was inspecting one of his father's far-flung plantations and other business interests.

Just two years earlier Henry Johnson and his wife, Elizabeth Flournoy, friends and neighbors, had produced their fifth child, who was christened Margaret Julia Johnson.

In her *Retrospect of Western Travel*, the nineteenth-century English author Harriet Martineau frequently mentions James and Anne Erwin, both in connection with her stay in New Orleans and in their steamboat voyages on the Mississippi.[1] In spite of her somewhat unfavorable critiques on America in general and mixed feelings about her stay in New Orleans, she seems to have had a lasting respect and friendship for the Erwins (designated in her book as "Mr. E" and "Mrs. E"). Of her friendship with Anne she notes after leaving New Orleans, "A friendship that I formed there, though already eclipsed by death, left me no feeling but rejoicing that I had gone."

Anne Clay, James Erwin's first wife, died in their house on Magazine Street in New Orleans on December 10, 1835; her son, Charles Edward Erwin, had been born some days before. Her mother, Lucretia, was with her as were James Erwin and their five other children: Julie D., Henry Clay, James, Jr., Lucretia, and Andrew Eugene. The household staff at this time consisted of a Miss Brulard, the governess for the girls, and the boys' tutor, a Mr. Richardson; three maids; a cook; a houseman; and two gardeners.

Henry Clay was in Washington at the time of Anne's death and he could not join the family when she was taken back to Lexington for burial. Julie and some of the younger children remained with Mrs. Clay. Miss Brulard accompanied them all to Kentucky, then returned "because she is homesick," wrote James to his father-in-law, continuing, "I will take the two boys back to New Orleans with me." Whether the children in Lexington were kept at Ashland by Lucretia Clay, as planned, or installed with nurses at James's house next to it, Woodlands, is not known.

Before leaving Lexington, James wrote to Clay in Washington a forlorn letter, here given in part:

1. Harriet Martineau became quite fond of Anne and James Erwin and she frequently mentions them in her letters to Henry Clay and in other writings. They met through Clay and she traveled with the Erwins up and down the Mississippi River on several of their many trips between Kentucky and New Orleans. Harriet Martineau, *Retrospect of Western Travel* (2 vols.; New York, Harper and Bros., 1838), I, 156, 220, 221, 276; II, 18, 21, 22.

The Woodlands
December 15, 1835

My dear Sir,

*I feel myself scarcely equal to the task which my duty imposes,
that of writing you at this time, and speaking of the late dreadful
calamity with which it has pleased God to inflict us—by which, at
the same fatal blow, has been taken from you a daughter, un-
equaled in filial devotion and love, and from me a wife, the most devoted, kind, and virtuous, with which ever man was blessed. . . .*

*Mrs. Clay [Lucretia], although in reality scarcely able to support
herself under this severe trial, has suppressed, as far as she was
able, her own feeling, intent only on rendering to me and my dear
children every kindness which her judgement and affection could
suggest. She has abandoned her own home and remained with us,
exerting herself to preserve the babe, which has cost us all so dear.
. . . [She] at once proposed taking charge of all of them, and have
Miss Brulard remove to Ashland, for the present, and teach them
as before. Miss B. wishes to return south, and the plan now is, to
leave the three youngest at Ashland, and the babe, with Lotty and
a wet nurse, under Mrs. Clay's care, and for the two boys, Henry
and James, to accompany me.*

*I expect to leave for New Orleans two days hence. My boys will
be important to me, and I shall take care not to let any feeling pre-
vent their having the best means for their improvement afforded
them.*

*I shall hope to hear from you very soon after I reach New Or-
leans.* [2]

It was apparent that throughout the years James was so devoted
to Anne (a devotion she returned), she had overlooked, ignored, or accepted his continuing relationship with one Rachel
L., of New Orleans, who had borne him two children. There is
some reason to believe that Henry Clay knew of this affair, ac-

2. This letter is in the Papers of Henry Clay, Perkins Library, Duke University.

cepting if not condoning it. The situation was not an unusual one.

For six years after Anne's death, James was busily occupied with his law firm in New Orleans (with offices in Nashville) and with his children, some of whom remained in Lexington. Aside from the interests of his immediate family, James remained close to his father-in-law, greatly concerned with him personally and with his interests. As early as 1833, Clay had begun to turn over to him matters concerning Ashland. In replacing an overseer, Clay wrote from Washington, "I will thank you to dismiss him and get another in his place. I should prefer a single man, but in that respect do the best you can. I am sorry to trouble you, but I know no one but you or Henry [Clay, Jr.] to whom I can address myself." And he signed himself "affectionately, H. Clay."

Besides this, James was engaged in looking after his own numerous plantations in Cahaba, Alabama, and Kentucky, and others in Mississippi, Arkansas, Louisiana, and Pennsylvania. He was a wealthy man and his second marriage to his distant cousin, Margaret Julia Johnson, of Fayette County, Kentucky, brought her own considerable wealth into the Erwin family. For the early part of her life—although not the youngest or eldest of the Johnson children—Margaret was a favorite of her father and of her Flournoy grandparents.

Henry Johnson was one of Kentucky's largest landowners and had married Betsy Flournoy (also called variously Eliza and Elizabeth), the third-generation daughter in America of Huguenot exiles who had fled France at the beginning of its eighteenth-century political upheaval, going first to Pennsylvania and then settling in Kentucky.

The Johnson family was on the unconventional side, to understate it, even for the times. Margaret's favorite uncle, Richard Mentor Johnson, was a Kentuckian who saw nothing out of the ordinary in keeping three mistresses, all slaves from his plantation, Blue Spring, not far from Lexington and Georgetown.

Two of these companions were coal black, while his favorite was the octoroon already mentioned, Julia Chinn. When he entered politics, first becoming a member of Congress, his family and friends tried to dissuade him from keeping this menage in action. His only answer was, supposedly, to dismiss the two black concubines and take Julia to Washington, where he first presented her to outraged society and then, reportedly, married her. They had two beautiful daughters, Imogene and Adeline. There was considerable political and social scurrying about the verbal attacks on him transcended libel. But in spite of everything, he became (by a vote of the Senate) vice president of the United States under Van Buren. Washington protocol must have had some hellish moments.

Most of the Johnsons never forgave him, nor did they forget Margaret's admiration of him. She thought that "Uncle Richard introduced the most *colorful* and jolly episode into this staid family since the serpent prodded Eve." She adored him and thus began a lifelong intra-family distancing, except from her sisters Louisa, Emily, and Mary Bell, and with one brother, Claudius Marcellus. They sided with her on almost every issue, then and later. Over the marriage and further eccentricities of Uncle Richard, the girls, when together, screamed with laughter.

But Richard Johnson was evidently a man much liked and one held in great respect before and during his political years. The style of his hair and the cut of his clothes raised many an eyebrow. And when, with time on his hands—as perhaps most vice presidents have had—he opened an inn just outside Washington, with he himself superintending even the cooking, Washington gave up. It was probably a simple and sinless way of passing the time while in an office that eventually became "quite tedious." (Yet not so much so that he did not try to win the post a second time around; in this he failed.)

Too, his politics were somewhat uncertain. He dangled over the fence, for he had a great personal regard for Abraham Lincoln and had "been a playmate of Mary Todd." He saw much of the Lincolns at home and then in Washington. This did not draw him closer to the bosom of the Johnson clan, as their great hopes lay in settling the burgeoning question of abolition through Stephen A. Douglas. Douglas, who became an intimate of Margaret's brother Matthew, she found offense in throughout her mature life and described as an "odious little creature." The word *odious* was to become her most disparaging label for anyone not in her favor.

James Erwin remained a widower for seven years and his decision to rewed was applauded by the Johnsons and Henry Clay himself, as well as by all the kith and kin that had settled around Kentucky's Fayette and Scott and Tennessee's McNairy counties. Margaret Johnson and James Erwin were married in Lexington[3] on February 21, 1843, at the Clays' Ashland, with Johnsons, Erwins, Wards, Breckinridges, Vileys, Sparks, Warfields, Dudleys, Worthingtons, Keenes, McKees, Sudduths, and Crittendens all at hand. It was reported as a "quiet" ceremony. The newlyweds immediately went to New Orleans.

The fact that Margaret had acquired a handsome, exuberant, wealthy husband almost twice her age, whose irons in the fire were not only countless but white-hot, did not seem to faze her. Neither money nor any other material thing had ever been a problem in her life, yet there is no indication of her being spoiled. (Later, her mother was to refute this.)

Margaret at first remained somewhat aloof from the younger Clay-Erwin children; she relegated them to tutors and governesses and the always ready and willing Lucretia Clay. After a few more years, Margaret would have the whole brood in the house in New Orleans, for it was a large, well-run establishment on Magazine Street, in what is still known as the Gar-

---

3. Family accounts had it that Margaret and James were married in Henry Johnson's house at Chatham, Mississippi; the sources are evenly divided, but, judging by the most reliable ones, the Kentucky wedding seems more logical.

den District. But from the first, the size of the place depressed her; it was a house whose aura or architecture she never wholly accepted.

Margaret found the New Orleans of the 1840s and 1850s much like Louisville—an exciting social merry-go-round of balls, theater, and music. She was amused for a time and missed Kentucky but slightly. But she thought "the quality of music in New Orleans and Louisville is not comparable. Louisville is much superior in this respect."

Little correspondence of Margaret Johnson Erwin has come down to us outside her letters to the elusive Carrie Wilson, to Samuel Sloan and his family, and to Eleanor Ewing (later Mrs. William Tecumseh Sherman), plus two letters to "Martha," and one to "Jennie." Carrie undoubtedly had much to do with Margaret's relationship and subsequent business dealings with the Sloans, while Eleanor was a friend whose husband was for a time the James Erwins' "financial advisor." This connection stems from New Orleans days, and even though Sherman apparently failed as a banker in California, Margaret continued to seek his advice until near her death.

The earliest complete letter I found was written to Carrie:

New Orleans
March 28 [1843?]

Dear Carrie,

    We are here at last. James seems happy, emotionally uncorrupted by the gloom that I, for one, would find in coming back to this house where he and Anne were so content, for so long, with their children. As for the younger ones, I adore them when I do not have to see too much of them—you know my feeling regarding children. They seem to have accepted me. I had feared that they would not; and Henry and Eugene are both growing into handsome men and seem most devoted (to me). James' work keeps him away much of the time.

*It seems that he must go to Nashville next week and Alabama
after that, all on business . . . too, his favorite Aunt, L. is sinking. It will be hard on him—and on Uncle I. Yet it is a thing we
must all face—prosaic, I know—but the brevity of all this—this
—all this—I do not know how to say it.*

And a few days later she wrote, "Miss Brulard is with us still,
and Mr. Richardson, who seems to be so good with the boys.
You remember that they were with Anne and James here during
the great tragedy." Still later, in the spring of 1843:

Carrie!

*I'm to have a child in the winter of next year! It is so good to
have Miss Brulard with us; she is a great comfort. Mr. Alison (a
new tutor) has his hands full with the boys—all so intelligent but
so full of spirit. [4] I am enjoying the music here and the gardens are
coming into their own—but I still feel a strange chill in the house.
It is all very grand and Magazine Street is a most perfect location.
Many of Anne's friends have called upon me; it is only by the
house that I feel rejected—I feel no part of it belongs to me. The
servants are of the best and I attribute Nettie getting over her
homesickness to their kindness to her.*

Nettie, a Negro, was Margaret's personal maid, or "body ser-
vant," and had been with her since both were children.

Henry Clay had an office in New Orleans—Clay and Brown
(Brown, a cousin)—and visited James and Margaret several
times, always staying at their house. The memories there must
have been difficult for him, too. Susan Duralde, another of
Clay's daughters, had lived in New Orleans and died there in
1825.

James, with his scattered interests, was a roving spirit and

---

4. I have never understood this reference to James and Anne's children, since they
were, by this time, mature or well on the way to maturity. In fact Henry Clay Erwin was
married.

New Orleans saw little of him. He was in the office for the more challenging business matters, but the rest was mostly left up to the junior partners. Occasionally Margaret would accompany James to her brother-in-law's house in Nashville when James headed in that direction. She always liked Nashville and found John Patton Erwin and his wife, Fanny (Williams), exceedingly hospitable. Too, there were Johnson cousins all around her. Most of these she found "most uncongenial." She did not elaborate, but she later remarked that "some of *my* relatives have all the vision and rigidity of a day old corpse."

After the birth of Julia Elizabeth (Lillie) in February, 1844, Margaret set out for Lexington, Philadelphia, and New York. She saw Carrie and many old friends. It was about this time that the idea of building a house of her own came to her. She discussed it with Samuel Sloan, who suggested that perhaps William Strickland would be the best architect for what he thought she had in mind. One supposes that he imagined all southerners wanted Greek temples, and since this was a Strickland specialty, probably he was the man. But not so. Strickland was not well, and a temple was the last thing in Margaret's mind. So Sloan played along with her but nothing was actually decided.

Having seen her father's plantations on Lake Washington, Mississippi, near Princeton (seat of Washington County at the time), she considered that probably somewhere within that region was a spot more to her taste than either Kentucky or the Gulf Coast. One of Henry Johnson's places, Mount Holly Plantation, with its then nondescript house, seemed attractive to her. She actually chose the land long before she acquired it; this was originally at her father's suggestion. The shabby building standing there could be torn down and a new one built; the surroundings were unkempt but had the makings of an English park, and with little effort could be made more so. Her father had said he would cooperate when she finally made up her mind.

24

She did come to a decision, but between the dream and the actuality came the birth of all five of her Erwin children.

A coolness between Margaret and her father was developing even before she came of age. The coolness with her brother Matt increased steadily and rapidly, particularly when he started entertaining Senator Douglas as a guest. When Douglas acquired land near Matt, he was even more in evidence. Then a wild word or two between brother and sister put up a barrier that never came down.

It was not until the last day of 1854 that Margaret bought Mount Holly Plantation from her father. The deed, dated December 30, 1854, is signed by Henry Johnson and his wife Eliza. The terms seem steep for the period: $100,000 for 1,900 acres of land, some uncleared, and a less than adequate house, "a desolate kennel of sticks and stones." But Margaret was looking ahead; much of her Lake Washington property was lakefront, bordered with cypress hundreds of years old. She had a vision and nothing was to dim it and prevent her from carrying out her still-nebulous plan.

When she was not pregnant, and in a few instances when she was, she traveled to England, to France, then once to Italy and Greece. The companionable Carrie was usually along. Most of the children were born in Kentucky, where she had Dr. Benjamin Winslow Dudley to rely on for care and advice. He was an eminent doctor of the time who specialized in (and innovated certain forms of) surgery—mainly lithotomy and an operation for cataracts. The Dudleys were to play an unexpected role later in her life.

Throughout the years of her marriage to James Erwin her world changed rapidly; but it was not only her world. When she headed north after Lillie's birth, Margaret for the first time showed some hesitancy regarding travel. She was disturbed at hearing of the steamboat *Shepherdess* running into some object in the Mississippi near St. Louis and sinking with the loss of more than fifty lives. "Imagine—in the middle of the night!" Shortly after, two boats collided in the river with eighty fatalities. Later, the boilers on the *Lucy Walker* exploded, and again there were more than fifty deaths.

They were years of considerable trepidation. There were rumors that Henry Clay had cut his political career to bits with his "Alabama Letter." He had previously stoutly denounced the annexation of Texas; in this modifying document he reneged and thereby lost all northern support. Margaret entertained many of James' and Henry Clay's friends and clients during her earliest years in New Orleans. But there were times when she was considerably thrown off her dignity by some of the characters that entered her drawing room.

To Carrie, [1844], from New Orleans

> *A most unpleasant evening. James brought my friend, William Sherman, to dinner and with them was a young man, a Lieut. Grant. The latter drank far too much and his attitude towards the coast—and whole south—proves that he should be sent back where he came from; his place is not here. I think William S. was much put out by his loudness and general behavior.*

Then she says, "for all his bluntness and unconcern with the arts William T. S. remains a gentleman; there is the occasional error in speech—but what is that in so excellent an advisor?" And attend her interests, and James Erwin's, he did, to the point of almost doubling their financial holdings. "WTS has suggested limiting our enterprises . . . ridding ourselves of certain properties here and certainly the unproductive place in Alabama."

Occasionally it is somewhat startling to find a well-known name mentioned casually in the letters, as in the following undated one to Carrie:

Thank you for that doleful but excellent poem, The Raven, *by the most despondent Mr. Poe. I felt quite motherly toward him when we met the one time. His is a most tragic story; I can only hope it ends well.*

And then, back to family matters:

To Carrie, February 14, 1844, from New Orleans

I have been seeing many old friends and making short excursions into the surrounding country. Of course, James' Uncle Joseph made quite a mark on this part of Louisiana (and in so doing made quite a fool of himself). [5] *But the remnants of his endeavors—well, some are too beautiful to be believed. . . [Some of them he held for only a brief period.] Part of the loss and desolation I feel due to bad planning. Poor Lavinia! and this hideous river can never be trusted—uglier water never existed.*

This was written at the same time she wrote the following letter to Eleanor Ewing:

I am fully recovered now and Julia Elizabeth, our first, is splendid. A very pretty child, so I am told, although all babies are alike as tennis balls. I feel so well that I am off to the opera one evening soon—Les Huguenots, I think.

These last few months have been most confining, but my friends have made it all quite gay for me—Mrs. Bourges, the Parkers, the DeGenerallys, the Pontalbas, the Pelletiers, and Destréhans—

5. James Erwin's uncle, Joseph Erwin, had gone overboard in his investments in Louisiana, after he and Lavinia left Tennessee. For a long time they paid him handsomely, but then came the depression of 1819 and in its aftermath some of his numerous plantations were lost. He went into a deep melancholia and his family persuaded him to take a trip by sea to Philadelphia. Under medical care he improved, but once back in Louisiana his troubles returned. One night he spent the night pacing the gallery of his home. The next morning he was found head down in a small cistern by the side of the house. He had drowned some time during the night. The family stuck by the story that it was an accident.

and, of course, the Robert Wards are here today, gone tomorrow, and then back again. [6]

The news from Kentucky is most disheartening what with the illness of Mr. Clay and Uncle Richard. Both have been spending much time in Washington, I understand. (To good use, I hope.) I have been interested in what I have heard of Samuel Morse (you remember we met twice when I was there) and I am delighted that his efforts and former disappointments are going to bear the right sort of fruit for him soon. I was much attracted to him and his Mr. Vail [Alfred Vail was an assistant to the inventor].

The controversy, the killing in Philadelphia, leaves me mindless: does religion, too much of it or the lack of it, always bring about fatal friction? I do hope my friends are not involved.

This last paragraph alludes to the riots that resulted from a dispute between Catholics and Protestants regarding the reading of the King James version of the Bible in schools. Over fifty were killed and many more injured, and as a result 5,000 militiamen were called to put an end to the fighting.

The next year again brought Margaret cause to think about limiting her regular mode of travel. The *Belle Zane* struck a snag and capsized, losing about half her passengers. In July, the *Marquette* boilers exploded and many people died. After a pause, and being wholly human, she relegated these tragedies to the back of her mind. Her courage was restored and she set out for Philadelphia and New York. About this time she decided that Sloan should definitely undertake the design and building of her house.

When Margaret made her first trip to London with Carrie, she amplified her already apparent anglophilia. She gave "Uncle

6. Besides the large town house in Louisville, the Robert Wards had a rather lavish establishment in New Orleans where he was co-owner of the firm of Ward and Jonas. The family divided their year between Kentucky and Louisiana, usually stopping for a few days at one of the family plantations in Tennessee, Mississippi, Arkansas, or Louisiana.

Henry" [Clay] credit for getting her family to unleash her when, as she says, most of her friends were "simpering ninnies with their mammy's milk still on their breath." There's a little of Scarlett O'Hara in that line. Had the one not been fiction, and had the two ever met, it would have been something akin to two great ladies walking into a ballroom of the period wearing the same Winterhalter gown.

Later she mentioned her (and Carrie's) chaperone, Miss Beam, and her suffering on that first English trip.

To Carrie, February 29, 1844

> *Do you remember the wild and ominous groans of poor Miss Beam crossing the ocean? I really think she could have been easily persuaded to stay in England forever rather than attempt the return trip.*

Her first voyage, although unrecorded by her at the time, so far as we know, was in the spring and summer of 1841, for afterwards she often mentioned "the English spring"; it occurred a year or so before her marriage and several years before her cousin Sallie Ward's marital interludes began.

Through Dr. Dudley, whose family was still connected with some of the oldest houses in England, she and Carrie managed to see many places not open to the general public. Lady Lyttleton was close to the "new" young queen, and saw to it that the two Americans met many interesting people. But Margaret says, several times, "I am never—never—impressed by position—it is the mortal frame that matters. That is, if guided by anything resembling a brain." This was the first trip abroad; thereafter she could never have enough of England. On later travels, after her marriage, Louisa or another of her two sisters always seemed to be glad to look after the children at the home in Kentucky or in New Orleans. James was away most of the time; she rarely mentions having any qualms about leaving him.

The rest of her family remained tight-lipped about her excursions (except Claudius Marcellus and her three sisters). By this time Margaret, although not the youngest in her large family, had her parents cowed and was in command of much respect from her siblings. They came to her first with any problems that called for sympathy or advice.

As the favorite granddaughter of the Flournoy antecedents, Margaret had inherited from them a considerable sum of money. From her seventeenth year on, her mother accused Henry Johnson of spoiling her "to a point of her never recovering." But while headstrong and determined to have her own way in things of importance, Margaret never showed the selfish preoccupation with feminine nonsense as pictured and practiced by so many southern girls of her time.

She always dressed extremely well and Nettie accompanied her on all her trips in America. She stayed in the best hotels, made friends easily and, it seems, was always among the most interesting people. But there was little or nothing of the snob in her. She was "devastated" at the sight of illness or poverty or old age, often in combination. No one will ever know the extent of her largesse; she was forever on tap for those less fortunate than herself.

However, this feeling did not extend to her own children; to them she gave all that she considered "sufficient for their needs . . . not more, for I will not have them grow into whining wretches and dissolute oafs." When the Clay-Erwin children were absorbed into the household, she wrote, "If only *our* children will grow into anything resembling the *ladies* and *gentlemen* that THEY are, from the eldest to the youngest."

The national picture began to cloud over: "expansion and intolerance and greed all in the name of necessity for the country's honor! How ridiculous! What honor?"

To Carrie, June 1846, from New Orleans

*Just as Mr. Clay said, it is happening [war with Mexico]. I hope
James has no preposterous ideas about heroism and the field of battle. There is quite enough of that to contend with here at home. I
am terrified to think that Henry Jr. will be in the midst of it.
[Henry Clay, Jr., was killed in the battle of Buena Vista the following year.]*

And:

To Carrie, August 1847, from Lexington

*No Cassandra, but I do go along with Father Henry regarding
the present conflict. Mexico has been in possession of Texas a
thousand years—what do we want with more land? We can not
offer any pattern for controlling what we have. We are not only
headed for the nearer disaster as a few of us can see, but beyond
that lies revolution. As for that, was it not Voltaire who said that
"no revolution can be termed successful until there is no one left to
judge it?" Well, I have my own opinions on what is going on in
Washington now—and will continue long after I have been taken
from this moribund society. What stupidities I am fed. There are
few things less profound than the sound of air escaping from an
inflated bladder or an expiring politician.*

The war with Mexico was to continue for a while longer, but
the American mind, having got itself involved with one matter, was (as was to become a matter of habit) being diverted by
another more pleasant vision: gold. It was discovered in California in 1849; by 1851 the annual output was assessed at $55
million. "What does it matter to those politicians in Washington that a few thousand lives are lost along borders of the far off
land of Texas?" Having prophesied the war and seen that his
was a losing argument, Henry Clay reluctantly returned to the
Senate after a "prolonged retreat" at Ashland. Once more in
Washington, some of his old fire flared up and he introduced
new measures for settling various matters. A Washington news-

paper tells of Clay's return in its report on an address he made before the Supreme Court:

> The courtroom was densely packed as never before. There were many ladies present and some of these even found standing places behind the bar, nearly crowding some of the justices off their stools. The magic manner of Henry Clay, the captivating tones of his voice and natural grace can never be transferred to paper. Mr. Clay exhibited as much vigor of intellect, clearness of elucidation, and power of analysis and legal research as he ever did. Perhaps there is no more remarkable example of the preservation of physical and mental faculties than Mr. Clay presents at this advanced period of his life. For three hours neither the voice of the speaker nor the interest of the listeners flagged.

Margaret wrote, "I hear that the scurrilous Grant is serving under General Taylor—why not present him to the Mexicans as a peace offering; THEY would know what to do with him—that *character*." This was to Eleanor Ewing, who married William T. Sherman in 1850. One wonders what eventually came of this friendship later, when both Grant and Sherman were set resolutely to the same cause.

After the loss of his son, Clay was a dejected man. Much of the time spent at Ashland was in a deep depression, over both personal problems and those of the country. Some pleasure was had from the proximity of his grandchildren at Woodlands, where the Erwins spent all their summers. But later he was again drawn back to Washington, much to the regret of his immediate family and particularly of Margaret; once there, he made his last attempt "to save the Union." This was his "compromise of 1850," but from the first he felt its eventual failure. In reviewing his own life, he must have sensed at times the seeming futility of watching over all that he cared about. Anne and Susan (Duralde) had died; one son had to be committed to an asylum; his namesake was killed in a war he had opposed. In all, six of his children died before his own death occurred.

In these last years he came to lean on James Erwin in matters of business advice and on Margaret and her children and step-children for any moral support to be had. Yet from the time of the declining effect of the "Compromise," he was seldom heard from. He died in Washington on June 29, 1852, just before the election of Franklin Pierce to the presidency; that he himself had failed to obtain that office was the final tragedy of a lifetime.

In July, 1846, although Margaret was expecting a child [Victor Flournoy Erwin was born October 18, 1846] in the fall, she went to New York. From there she wrote Carrie, "In spite of my *condition* I feel exceptionally well. William [Templeton] Johnson is to be married to Laura Winthrop; I am very happy about this. A dear girl. I met George Strong at the dedication or consecration or whatever at Trinity Church; the music was on the puny side."

On an earlier trip to New York Margaret reported another encounter with Lieutenant Grant:

> I could not make out one word he said, he was so inebriated. He stepped on Mrs. Spangler's gown, tearing the hem, and then almost fell to the floor. She was outraged and went from the room and would not return until some gentleman had escorted the belching donkey from the house. Seton was among them and when he returned he only shook his head; no comment.

Margaret had been attracted to Sherman and obviously had taken an immediate dislike to Grant. One wonders at her perceptiveness in this, not so much at her intuition regarding Grant but that none of Sherman's ruthlessness-to-come showed at this time. Grant is another matter. Much later than Margaret's day, when Grant was president, even some of his own friends and cabinet had little to say for him. His secretary of state, Gideon Welles, said that he "has no regard for dignity or human life . . . and is a fool." Margaret did not live to see Grant as commander of Union forces, either; nor did she see the violence

33

that Sherman wreaked in his famous march to the sea. At one time, she wrote Eleanor, "I envy the astuteness and acuity of your husband." She felt strongly that those qualities in themselves were something that Grant sorely lacked. "Travel is supposed to do wonders for one," Margaret wrote to Carrie in 1847, "but I feel free to say that the dreary little lieutenant [Grant] has not profited by it . . . but then, except for a brief sortie to the east and south coasts, he has hardly left the region of the midwest; he was a renegade at West Point. Whatever Julia [Dent, whom Grant married the following year] sees in him is apparently invisible to others."

To Carrie, [1846?], from Lexington

A few nights after the disgraceful Grant-Spangler affair we took tea with a most dreary woman, a Mrs. Devine. Mrs. Beekman was there and we had many sly looks (in fact it was commendable that we kept a straight face). We met the next day and laughed outrageously at the insufferable stupidity and pretentiousness of Mrs. D. May I be spared further contact in this world with that woman. Jane Beekman and I both admitted that our own behavior was far from correct—and then went into further spasms of laughter. Who is to know?

I have been to several concerts—one or two VERY SMALL in every respect, but each time to a disgustingly large dinner afterwards. I shall be quite ready for the tranquility of the Lake—and, of course, I will have the delightful hours with you and the dear Sloans of Philadelphia.

The year following the birth of her son Victor, Margaret wrote Eleanor:

I know you will say it is "just war" but I can not forgive anyone for the death of Henry C. Jr. His father foretold this dreadful affair and says the worst for this country's greed and obstinacy

*has not yet come! God help us, in that case. Dear love to you and
yours,*

M.J.E.

Early in 1847, Margaret again spent some months in the East.
This time she toured with grim determination, seeing every
available architectural "gem." She was not satisfied with either
the "chateaux" of the *nouveaux riches*, nor with the beauty or
simple dignity of many of the houses of "fishwives and witch
hunters." Her displeasure must have placed Samuel Sloan in a
quandary. But his tastes were cosmopolitan, and finally his pro-
jection of what struck her as a romanticized version of an "Italian
Villa" caught her fancy. After some thought and dawdling, and
hundreds of preliminary sketches, she decided: this was what
she would have. No columns, no ersatz bits of Brittany and Nor-
mandy—a villa. "No temples—I hardly consider myself a ves-
tal virgin!"

To Carrie, [Winter ?] 1847, from New Orleans

*We went to a most lavish ball at one of the neighboring planta-
tions—Gentilly—and met many old friends. There are times
when I think that life here is but dancing in half time, slow, grace-
ful, gentle. And then I went to my Lake again.*

*But the ball was splendid and we are planning one for Magazine
street later in the season before the morbid onslaught of Lent. It
would not make much difference except Catholic New Orleans is
so annoyingly devout, and this includes so many of our friends. I
shall go home. Then I shall come back for this party and then to
New York. Later I shall return here again for the opening of the
Metairie season.*

The Metairie racing season was one that was equalled only by
Ascot and Doncaster in England. It was attended by the public
from all over the states; the actual membership was exclusive.

The entries included the finest horseflesh the country had to offer. Later, Margaret's daughter Lillie and her husband, Oliver Morgan, were members, as was James Erwin (he being a leading breeder of horses). A subscription receipt is among existing papers.

To Carrie [1847], from New Orleans

> *We visited the old plantation for the last time. I think that both Jacob and James are tired of wrestling with the river. It can only be wearing and result in eventual loss.*

The "old plantation" refers to one of several of the Louisiana lands along the Red River and in the Caddo country, acquired plantation by plantation by Joseph Erwin from 1800 on, and later by his nephews, James and Jacob Erwin, late in the 1830s and 1840s. As a prophetic example, their Uncle Joseph had overextended himself, winding up with his dozen or so vast tracts of land, a house of some size and beauty on each and, even after passing one after another on to his children as they married, he held on to enough to bring about his eventual financial downfall. He died a suicide after struggling to regain some part of his losses, and failing.

After his death, his widow, Lavinia, took up the torch. But the first successes were never again quite realized. Yet when Lavinia died in 1836, her probated will shows a net worth of $262,105. This is entirely due to her diligence, as Uncle Joseph left the estates entailed for almost $500,000.

The year 1847 also found Margaret shuffling through a mass of house plans. She remained in Lexington, unsettled in mind, restless in spirit. She knew that she must have a place soon to consolidate her expanding family. "Time," she said, "is not forever."

Margaret and James's son, James, was born in October of 1848. (He lived but one month.) She was in Lexington for this event and there is a short excerpt from a note to Carrie that would have much bearing on the future. "I hear that Matilda (Viley) Ward, cousin of Junius' wife, has just given birth to a girl. They are at the old place and will remain there for some time." This daughter, also christened Matilda, would eventually marry Margaret's third son, Johnson Erwin. The fact that Matilda was two years older than her husband was always to remain a not-very-well kept (and deeply resented) secret; the date of her birth is carefully cut from the family Bible.

Margaret was an avid reader, concerned greatly with the literary past and with her current literary world. When some new luminary intruded on her consciousness everyone soon knew about it. It appears that she read French and Italian with ease.

[To?], from Lexington

> . . . have just read Eugene Onegin in French by one Alexander Pushkin. Extraordinary for its realism and nostalgia. . . the "great" may have been misapplied to Catherine for her identification with the naughty Orloff brothers, and Baldassare Galuppi. Yet what music came of the latter!

In 1848, during the early summer there was a family tragedy that is not mentioned in any family records: James Erwin, Jr., son of Anne and James, committed suicide in the St. Charles Hotel in New Orleans. The family scuttled the facts in the case to such a degree that there is no documented evidence available, either to the act or the motives behind it. James II is buried in Lexington near his father, and not far from Anne. These are the only references that we have from Margaret, dates unknown:

> The tragedy is unexplained. It was not gambling and it was not drinking for he had not been doing much of that of late. Two friends had been with him and one was there when he heard the shot. No apparent reason. J. Jr. always a complex, remote boy.

James has not been the same since the affair in the hotel in New Orleans. He was always perplexed by J. Jr. but always felt some kindred concern—closer than father and son. He is most depressed and goes north next week.

To Carrie, August 2, 1848

I am more impressed as time goes on by the facts that have come to me regarding the school for Indians that Uncle Richard founded in Kentucky. Whether it is an act of conscience (for his supposedly killing Tecumseh—I have never believed that nor heard it from him) or his usual compassion for people of no privilege I do not know. In any case, it is admirable—and considering what we have done to those people and their lands.

The crafts school that Richard M. Johnson had founded near his home in Kentucky was the first of its kind to attempt to consolidate the skills of the white man with those of his red "brothers."

Very early in 1848, Margaret had toyed with the idea of another trip to England and France, but in November she wrote Carrie:

Pregnant again . . . and the troubles of the French are most disconcerting. The Tuilleries ruined by the mob, so we hear, and thousands killed. What a bloody race the French have once more turned out to be, and now they speak of a republic.

And a republic they did have, for as long as it lasted: Napoleon III became president on December 20. Margaret had her say:

Have we not had enough examples of them? Democracy—Republic—what do they all mean—words, words, words!

By December of that year she had fully recovered her energies and enthusiasms; death was tragic, death was unfair, but there were so many of the living to be dealt with.

Part II—1843–1851

To Carrie, December 19, 1848, from New Orleans

*In spite of little James' death [Born October, 1848; died a
month later] we go on. Christmas has become such a ravening
season, so far removed from its intent and beginning. But James
and the children make much of it—even as I suppose we did in
Kentucky. There were so many of us and we were such gay ones!
I go along with the hustle and mayhem of it all. Yet now that we—
and I do mean we—brought the "Christmas tree" from England,
I am in constant terror as far as fire is concerned (candles, at best,
are a menace), but then I think that there is little danger here in the
marble tomb, except there are draperies, rugs, tapestries, and furniture coverings.*

She added a postscript, referring to the Christmas tree:

*I understand that the English adapted it from the Germans—
those tasteless swine—and that they got it from the Romans.*

*I, for one, was content with being a Druid with my mistletoe
and holly berries, but I suppose there is too much of the Saxon in
all of us.*

> [same letter]
> December 20, 1848
> *Italy has got herself into an uproar—papacy, as for centuries
> (same as Baptists for all I care) at the bottom of it all. Count
> Rossi, that wonderful man, was made [papal] prime minister.*

To Carrie, February 1849, from New Orleans

*. . . the Pope ineffectual as all these great creepers from between
the stratifications of the ages—the great Rossi assassinated!!!
[November 15, 1848] The Holy One (Terror as far as I am concerned) has flown the trap—disappeared to somewhere near
Naples. Cowardly and obtuse.*

Margaret was again to see an early spring in England in 1849, while an ailing James went to Pennsylvania on business. In Philadelphia (he reported to her later), Mr. Rittenhouse and Mr. Sloan had·asked why he had never considered following the course of so much of his family and entered politics. Margaret's response was: "I fear that his answer may have greatly shocked them, for he said that to do so would be like a healthy man walking into a burning house at a point where the roof is about to cave in—and not letting that be the end of it, he further said that after H[enry] C[lay] and Mr. W[ebster] are gone there would be no men in public office he would trust unless it be Lincoln."

James's opinion of Douglas and the other opponents and detractors of Abraham Lincoln was another point he fully shared with his wife. "James says that instead of trying to live up to our Constitution, those swindlers in Washington are merely trying to riddle and exploit it. He says the other gentlemen saw his point. Yet I wonder."

Of her travels (with Carrie again) she wrote Eleanor later in the year:

To Eleanor, October 17 [1849]

I did see my cousin, again in England, Lady L. (the one you met and liked so much), and it was she who arranged for us to see Windsor (her cousin is a lady-in-waiting to the Queen). I wanted very much to see the castle but I was not prepared that it should be arranged for us to have tea with HM and Prince Albert. At first I was greatly put out, as I am not a great admirer of Germans, as you well know. After what seemed an endless trip through a light rain (it did clear while we were indoors, thank God) I found in HM all that I would expect.

We were early and waited half an hour for the proper time, lodged in a room that seemed to be in a state of renovation (one can only hope); I am convinced that Their Majesties were doing exactly the same thing on the other side of the door; the whole thing could have been got over within half the time. After all, I was not there for human companionship and I am not impressed by people—I was there to see the palace.

I can only hope I did not show my annoyance. Had I kept Her waiting, I can imagine my reception. In any case, I did not curtsey well. I still insist brainless debutantes do it best (and female dogs when relieving themselves). But I bowed and was given the Royal hand and a friendly smile. She is not an attractive woman, nor is she ugly. If one ever got to know her one would find petulance and hysteria, but her earlier life was not easy and Albert was certainly a godsend to the nation. I may even have to retract some of my opinions regarding the Germans as a people. The Prince was most courteous and while neither of them ever discuss politics —national or international—(so I was warned) they did inquire most minutely into my knowledge of what is going on in America, particularly as to the question of abolition.

Her Majesty was most pleasant throughout, and after our American discussion we finished tea in an ocean of verbal nonentities. She wished me to see much of Windsor and since she was indisposed the Prince escorted us through many dark corridors-without-end and into some rooms —mostly filled with unspeakable brick-a-brac. I did not see the archives or library. After leaving Their Majesties, Lady L. took us to the beautiful little Elizabethan court and to the exquisite Chapel; there I could live.

In this, one of the longest of Margaret's letters, she added, almost as an afterthought:

Her Majesty was most gracious but at times a rather grim and humorless young woman. Hers is a great burden; but there are different manners in which to carry such. Her moods seem to be much dreaded; one would think the Tudors were back with their "off-with-their-heads" whims. All in all it turned out pleasantly, and when we emerged from what I expected to be a rather tiresome experience (looked back upon), we were greeted by a bright sun

*and a tour, an endless tour, of beautiful Windsor Park. The castle
may be grim (the* odors *sometimes are most unpleasant—what
can this be? And so little noticed; perhaps a royal nose is not as
acute as ordinary humans) but the Park is completely magnificent!*

Cecil Woodham-Smith, in her *Queen Victoria*, has a fascinating reference to the question of Windsor's odors:

> The splendour of Windsor concealed dangers. In 1848 the Lord
> Chamberlain reported to the Department of Woods and Forests
> that the works most urgently required for the safety of Windsor
> Castle were the completion of the drainage, begun in 1846. The
> main drains had then been constructed "but nothing was then or
> has since been done to improve the drains in connection with the
> various water closets, sinks etc. within the Castle. The noxious ef-
> fluvia which escapes from the old drains and numerous cesspools
> still remaining is frequently so exceedingly offensive as to render
> many parts of the castle almost uninhabitable, and scarcely any
> portion can be said to be entirely free from the effects of imperfect
> drainage. It is therefore highly desirable that the completion of the
> work should be recommenced. . . ." Beneath the splendour, Wind-
> sor Castle was more dangerous than a jungle.[7]

And later Mrs. Woodham-Smith refers to a letter from Dr. William Jenner to a doctor friend: "'My dear Parkes,' he wrote, 'the
Prince of course had typhoid fever . . . .' The drains of Windsor Castle, condemned years ago and never put in order, had
proved more dangerous than a tropical jungle."

The antipathy toward Germans felt by Margaret Erwin remains something of a mystery that only a Jung or an Adler might
explain. She had never been subjected to the company of many;
she adored Italians and Greeks, admired the French and thought
them charming but "often fools." Of the Spanish (of whom she
knew not a few in New Orleans), "they are quite wooden, and

7. Cecil Woodham-Smith, *Queen Victoria* (New York: Alfred A. Knopf, 1972),
279.

their music gives me a headache." But Germans? There is a hint in one of her letters that it could have begun as a family matter when one of her brothers became engaged to a Miss Frida Bauer; whether he married her is unrecorded. But Margaret never spoke to him or of him again, in any case. He was known among the first members of the Johnson family to be *persona non grata* in her house—in any she ever occupied. But he should not have felt lonely; there were to be quite a few others to keep him company— namely, their father, Henry, and her brother Matthew.

Yet whatever her opinions of the British monarch on personal grounds, Britain has seldom had a greater American admirer. Whenever the subject of the American Revolution was mentioned, Margaret, according to her daughter-in-law Matilda, "gave loud and most theatrical groans." She was a vat-dyed monarchist at heart and held the opinion that "of that whole U.S. medley, only Jefferson deserved to be heard. He was our greatest. Washington was a military ninny . . . perfectly content with that hausfrau."

She writes to Eleanor of her trip to Greece:

To Eleanor, September [1849], from New Orleans

> *The trip to Greece was somewhat of a nightmare and I am afraid Carrie was worried about my delicate condition. But we made it. Athens: absolute squalor. The Acropolis all I expected, and other ruins. Then I had to go to Delphi, and because of my disappointment regarding Mt. Athos, Carrie sighed deeply and let me have my way. Such roads or trails! I slipped from my donkey and sat heavily on my derriere—and Carrie came near to hysterics. I got up laughing (more for her benefit than mine) and we finally got there. There is something quite awesome about Delphi. I have seen the Alps, most of them, but I think Lycabettus, Hymettus, Parnassus, and Mt. Olympus have an aura no other mountains have. There is such magic about Delphi that I can no longer disbelieve in the Greek gods. No great luck with the Oracle but I did*

wash a bit in the Castalian spring, that I may be brought back to Greece. But Greece's poverty—I can not speak of it.

Margaret went abroad only once more, in 1850, for the tremors of her own world increased for the next twelve years and then brought it down about her. Of that last trip little or nothing is known.

As to her reference to Mount Athos: after making all her plans to visit there, as to each and every hour, she found that women were not welcome at the monastery. In fact, they were not allowed to proceed up the mountain itself. For this, Margaret always was petulantly silent when the subject was mentioned.

After Greece, they went to Capri where she thought "Tiberius could only have been a gay and likable fellow—with this sea, this panorama; I could live here forever." They sailed from an Italian port and "had a quiet trip through the Mediterranean, and thrilled at the sight of the Balearic Islands and then Gibraltar."

And again to Carrie:

To Carrie, December 12, 1849, from New Orleans

I do not mean that I shall never speak to you again if you ever intimate what a frolic our trip really was! Much stands out in England that is unforgettable, among this the concert by Miss Lind and Mr. Mendelssohn. I admit I expected more of a voice, which I found most shrill. But Mr. Mendelssohn was all that I expected. I can understand the Queen's seeming infatuation, although I still have to admit to not understanding much else about her. Such a hausfrau! And the Prince—so handsome.

I can hardly wait to tell L M G [Louis Moreau Gottschalk] about the music we heard.

Please thank Mr. Sloan for arranging for us to see as much of Hampton Court as we did. As for Paris

Here the letter ends, for the next page is missing. However, two days later she tells Eleanor Ewing what may possibly be lost in the missing fragment:

> *The last evening in Paris was most rewarding. A most amazing new play by Scribe,* Adrienne Lecouvreur—*the role being played by Rachel, that superb actress! I had seen her only once before, in* Phedre; *this time, as last, incomparable. What a poverty of the good and great things we experience in America. Opera in New Orleans is a delight, to have it so close at hand. Yet it sometimes resembles the sounds coming from choir stalls as compared with London and New York.*

Continuing, after still another missing page:

> *I found myself thinking of being so far from home. I knew for certain that I was pregnant by the time I got off the ship in England. And that was disturbing. Yet the everyday events catch one up, as in a whirlwind, and one becomes blind even to the bothersomeness of pregnancy. Paris was unsettled; there seemed no sense of direction and the government seems as unstable as our own. I saw N. III [Louis Napoleon] at a ball, was presented—but pshaw, what an oaf! De Chaumont gave us all of his time and seemed to relish our company—me at my age! [She was then 28.]*

Another letter to Carrie, of uncertain date:

To Carrie, [December ?] 1849, from New Orleans

> *I have just heard of the death of M. Chopin [October 17, 1849]. I can only think of the concert in the Salle Pleyel, and the utter frenzy following it. Such magnificent music! I now, in my own sadness, can think of what the loss will mean when young Louis [Gottschalk] hears of it. To think we were among the "anointed" to hear M. Chopin and F. Liszt . . . one the poet, the other a cannonade—yet both made of music, the only lasting art.*

And to Carrie again on the same subject, undated:

> *. . . to think we heard both M. Chopin and F. Liszt the same year —Chopin in Paris and Liszt in Rome. It is indeed sad to think that one so young [Chopin] was cut off in perhaps his greatest years, although, God knows, his was a gift among gifts.*

It was during that Parisian adventure that Margaret met Ferdinand Marie de Lesseps, "a charming man but somewhat preoccupied regarding what the Church of Rome will do or say on that or the other question." This was the Vicomte de Lesseps who, in 1859, would commence his great work, the Suez Canal, in the same year during which Margaret would witness the completion of Mount Holly. She had known his cousin, Alexander de Lesseps, in New Orleans.

[To ?], June 1849

> *F. de L. [Ferdinand de Lesseps] has gone trundling around with a fist full of signatures for the Romans—to what end I can not surmise. One, Garibaldi, has made far more headway in solving the problems and keeping Italy intact.*

A similar encounter is referred to in a letter addressed to "Jennie."

To Jennie [1849], from London

> *. . . and last night a reception at Lady L's where I met several delightful people. One aging gentleman took an obvious interest in me and talked much of America and of Alexis's [de Toqueville] opinions of our government—the "most salient views since Jefferson"; I could but agree. A little later I found out that he was the Duke of Wellington. It quite took me by surprise.*

And another from London that same year, but it is not known to whom it was addressed:

*It has been a most rewarding experience, meeting so many peo-
ple with whom I disagreed and now —hearing them, rather than
reading them—seeing their position. And quite the reverse has
occurred, too. In any case, the list is a lengthy one and someday I
shall tell you about them: Mr. Disraeli, John Forster, William
Wordsworth, Thomas Carlyle, Richard Monkton Milnes and
Henry Hallam and so many more.*

*Leaving England will be leaving a country of pride and integrity
for the poor shambles that my own has become. Would that I could
persuade James to establish himself here—it would be by no
means impossible. I should miss New York, Philadelphia, and
Louisville—and the Lake (the same shadow of hesitation, almost
foreboding still hovers when I think of it) but this beautiful country
would soon cure me, perhaps even of too much memory. And I
should not miss our political gyrations.*

Margaret was home again by November of 1849:

To Eleanor, November 26, 1849, from New Orleans

*James brought the B. de P. by to see the "winter" gardens. She
was much impressed, even as I was by her plans for the square in
front of the Cathedral. I must still tell you of our trip and the com-
plexities.*

The "winter garden" attached to the house on Magazine Street
was much admired in New Orleans; one of Margaret's great interests had always been horticulture, an interest that went with
her to Mount Holly but never found full fruition there. The
guest mentioned above was obviously the Baroness de Pontalba,
who was responsible for the creation of Jackson Square and the
building of the architectural masterpieces, the Pontalba Apart-
ments, that flank it and provide a beautiful setting for St. Louis
Cathedral.

In spite of the preparation for the holidays and the birth of her child early in the year (Johnson, born March 22, 1850), Margaret seemed more in a letter-writing mood than ever, although the above two sentences to Eleanor Ewing were put aside for two weeks, then returned to:

Yes, it was true—and I thought at first that I had merely carried my seasickness ashore with me. But I was determined to continue as planned and we did so. From Paris we went to Rome where I was fascinated by the vast piles of stone . . . so neglected. I bought an antique head, quite beautiful, by way of Dr. Paglio. He also made an appointment for me to see the last living Medici, and when the day arrived we found the old lady had died the night before. I was most put out. Then I learned that Anna Marie Ludovica Medici, the last legitimate one, had died in 1743, and this lonely old soul was illegitimate. Well, it would have been better to meet an illegitimate Medici than none at all. I sent flowers to the church, God knows why. In Paris I bought enough clothes to last me the rest of my life, foolish woman that I am—and I will not be able to wear them until I get over this period of lumbering around like an ancient, bloated buffalo. My portrait done—in crimson—by F. X. Winterhalter, the artist of the moment. Must leave the gown, as he has had but time to paint in my face and hands . . . at least the fact that I am enceinte will not show.

She wrote to Eleanor early in the spring of 1850, a few months after Johnson's birth:

No, I won't even say it. I have sworn to James that I shall not be involved in politics from here on.
America is doomed—utterly doomed, although it may take a century of wallowing in the filth of political ambitions to prove it.
We are headed for ruin, wearing blinders, what with all this agitation, there is not a man alive with gumption enough to save us, unless it be my two failing dear ones [Henry Clay and Daniel

*Webster]. Outside of Alexander the Great or Marlborough I can-
not think of a dead one.*

*I have been out of sorts and too unwell this past winter, and
there have been some complications. I sometimes wonder if I
should have married at all, when I stop to consider it. I like the idea
of progeny, but I really dislike children until they become sensible
enough to cease being "darling" (to others) and stop their eternal
prattling, and at birth they always look like something that has
been discarded as part of the lion's dinner. Their nurses and tutors
should be paid double for putting up with all their whining and
nonsense and tantrums.*

To Eleanor, [Summer 1850]

*I am very happy for you. Martha [see p. 68] wrote me of the
"event." I have ever been an admirer of your husband and have
long known of his devotion to you and your family . . .*

This is in regard to Eleanor Ewing's marriage to William Tecumseh Sherman on May 1, 1850; Sherman had been adopted into
the Ewing family as a boy and thus was Eleanor's foster brother.

One of the members of the Sloan office in Philadelphia saw
Margaret in New Orleans. Again she was undecided about putting her plan into effect. But on going to Philadelphia that summer, she arrived in a more settled state of mind. On her way
north she had stopped in Nashville for a week, then in Lexington and Frankfort, and visited "a multitude" of relatives.

*. . . some of them are just too irritating to be around for long, and
some are so common, so mundane in their tastes and views, I believe there was something quite untidy going on behind the barn
and they are not relatives at all. Of course, we all have real relations better left unmentioned.*

Yet this was a year in which, in Philadelphia, she gathered up

Carrie and they set off to England. Although the tour was of some months duration, little or nothing is known of the details.

It was on this prolonged European trip that the culmination of the plans for Mount Holly began. She had almost approved the plan of a "semi-Italian" villa, "just so it doesn't have tiles on the roof." She had come even more to the conclusion that she must consolidate her family at last. Woodlands,[8] the Kentucky house that had belonged to James and Anne, depressed her; the same thing was true of the house in New Orleans. There were three family homes on Lake Washington and, of course, she and James had long had their eyes on Henry Johnson's Mount Holly Plantation. The existing house stood on high ground, surrounded by live oaks, pin oaks, and other great indigenous trees. It was precisely where she wanted to build. Her father and mother had long seemed agreeable to letting her have the plantation of some 1,900 acres and a wide area of lake front.

Back to Carrie, with some political thoughts.

To Carrie, [1850], from Lexington

I have been impressed by reading of the visionary trends in Europe. Perhaps if we had a few men like Herzen and Bakunin to augment our weak-kneed stalwarts (and the real ones like Clay and Calhoun and Webster) we would be able to put lightweights like Douglas in their proper place (a dungeon preferably).

Also were I in charge of making the list I would confine father,

8. Since the James Erwin occupancy, Woodlands (ca. 1830) served as a building of the State Agricultural College when it was established as part of the University of Kentucky. It was razed in the early part of the century, the grounds becoming Woodland Park. Clay Lancaster (*Ante Bellum Houses of the Bluegrass* [University Press of Kentucky, 1961] says "the bizarre elements of Woodlands were the octagonal flankers capped by wooden bonnets with baroque finials. . . . It is possible that the Woodlands appendages were later additions to the original house. Octagonal garconieres were common in Louisiana, Erwin's home state. Although the effect of Woodlands lacked refinement it cannot be said to have been without distinction." More personal family history has it that James Erwin, being a breeder of race horses among his other activities, had the simple finials replaced with carved heads of his favorite horses. Distinction Woodlands may have had, but there is some doubt as to the owner's taste if this is true.

Mat, Harriet B. S. [Beecher Stowe], and Mrs. Lum, and there are several others! How I despise little common narrow minds! They have set the world on edge and we have not seen the last of their influence yet.

Michael Bakunin, a founder of Russian revolutionary socialism, is called the "father of anarchy." Herzen's activities were in accord with those of Bakunin; he lived mainly in Paris and London. It's fortunate that Margaret kept her opinions within her own country. Anarchy in Europe was making headlines in her time and just beginning its slow roll westward. In any case, Margaret was never far removed from politics. She was as sensitive to international causes and upheavals as she was to the disorder that she saw rising in her own country—often with bitter but accurate insight.

To Samuel Sloan, [early] 1851, from New Orleans

We have discussed the possibility of taking part of one of the B. de P's [Baroness de Pontalba's] new building. I only think of the children—there would no longer be the vast garden, nor would they feel the same living so close to others. The "others" might have something to say about that themselves. For the B. de P. I have developed a great affection, a most remarkable and active woman. I wonder if you are familiar with the architect of her houses, James Gallier? I do not know how my James would feel about awakening to find the proposed statue of Andrew Jackson [proposed 1850, completed 1851] rearing up at him every morning; you know the Jackson-Erwin points of difference.

The Cathedral remains an edifice of gloom and I do not see how De Pouilly's addition to it can remedy a most grievous mistake that was made in the first place.

Margaret always felt an antipathy towards the Cathedral of St. Louis; de Pouilly merely added fuel to her criticism when he put steeples on it and changed the facade in 1851.

James (he is most unwell, but I am assured there is no cause for alarm) can set up a bachelor nest for himself to use when he has court, or he can go with. . . .

To this interrupted letter, one can only suppose (in the light of other documents) that she would have added, "his mistress Rachel." Margaret never seemed to have qualms about her own, legal hold on James nor does she ever express any animosity or jealousy about his association with other women (and she knew there were others). Yet their relationship was certainly more than one of polite affability.

Although Margaret mentions the decision to sell the New Orleans house, nothing came of it that spring. In January, 1851, the "dream house" in Mississippi was much on her mind.

To Samuel Sloan, January 10, 1851, from Lexington

I have returned to Kentucky for a few months. My son Johnson (born last March) has not proven to be the healthiest of infants. I am consulting Dr. Benjamin Dudley. The improvement in J's condition is already quite amazing. I expect to return south within the next two weeks.

But she did not go home. Instead, settling Johnson with Kentucky relatives, she proceeded on to New York. To Carrie: "most rewarding, this unexpected trip to New York. Some business to be seen to, and many old friends. Whether one is justified in traveling at all these days is quite a question; the number of accidents by boat and by train is appalling. A pleasant evening with Mrs. Suydam who was most anxious for news of you; much amusement over the Rochester rappings affair."

The "Rochester rappings" affair was a hoax involving two girls of the Fox family of Rochester, New York. Mysterious sounds and unexplained phenomena when they were present attracted much publicity. New York became goggle-eyed over the matter and the girls were brought to the city. The whole matter proved a most remunerative one until Margaret Fox admitted the "happenings" were false. For one thing the mysterious sounds were made by cracking her toes! The girls allegedly were able to communicate with ghosts, poltergeists, nincompoops, and the Almighty. Even the earthy Horace Greeley gave the matter much space in the *Tribune*, thus giving spiritualism a boost. One wonders what Greeley's reaction was when the hoax was exposed. The abrupt close of this comment was unusual and attracted my attention:

> *I saw Mr. Strong—William's cousin and he is as dubious as I regarding the Rochester phenomena. Met the Bishop of Jamaica; not impressed, quite the reverse . . . I must go home soon.*

She did go to New Orleans, picking up her son in Lexington on the way, and stopping in Nashville for a few days. She always seemed to find her Erwin relatives there "acceptable and pleasant."

Some change in James must have become obvious at this point. It wasn't "old time religion," for he was not one who would make more than the most outward motions towards a nebulous (he said) "other world and a regrettable bit of mythology." Did Rachel find a younger (certainly not wealthier) lover in New Orleans? This may be so, for James spent less time there, appearing in court only for the more important cases. But even if there had been a change in Rachel's affections, it doesn't seem that it should have bothered James to any great extent. New Orleans of the time was a cosmopolitan world of beautiful, attractive women. Yet he now spent more time in Lexington with Margaret and they pored for hours over the plans for the house that she planned to build on Lake Washington.

They had never quite agreed on what type of house it should be, but she was assured of having her own last word by bearing the full cost. James leaned towards any one of several comfortable plantation houses that his Uncle Joseph had built in Louisiana, one after the other, and at times he was all for a "Greek temple" (but Margaret had already aired her views on that, so there was little more to be said about them). Margaret's ideas had been gathered around the country and in England, and in Samuel Sloan she had a kindred spirit: "the house must be large and comfortable, unique in its elegance and beauty." In Sloan she had a man who was pliant and possessed a sense of fantasy as well. (Note Longwood[9] in Natchez; see illustration.)

For nearly ten years Margaret had visited the Philadelphia home of the Sloans and corresponded with Sloan regarding her future house. Plans—whole, some torn to bits—were many and traveled the long distance between Lexington and Philadelphia. For all their architectural disagreements, Margaret and the Sloans remained close friends.

During the summer of 1850 James Erwin's health had grown worse, but in spite of that he had made the trip to New Orleans. While there he was stricken with some additional ailment, never identified as more than "a light case of the fever." As this followed none of the usual disastrous patterns of yellow fever, it is doubtful that his illness was more than one of his increasing "digestive attacks." Yellow fever was of such virulence that one seldom came down with it and ever got up again. Some weeks later he arrived on Lake Washington, "tired and worn looking —there is nothing of the old James about him."

He was fifty-five and had always enjoyed superb health; now he was "restless and irritated." He crossed to Arkansas and to Shreveport (Louisiana) to look over some lands he had acquired there in 1837. Then he returned to one of the Johnson houses near Chatham (Mississippi) feeling worse than before. Finally he consented to go to Nashville, possibly Kentucky, "when the

9. Longwood, built by Samuel Sloan for Dr. Haller Nutt was never completed. Dr. Nutt died in 1864 and his wife and children occupied the ground floor. It was owned by his descendants, Mrs. Robert Blanchard, Mrs. James Ward, and Mrs. Leslie K. Pollard until it was sold in 1968. The buyers, Mr. and Mrs. Kelly E. McAdams of Texas presented the house to the Pilgrimage Garden Club of Natchez, Mississippi.

weather changes." But the doctors in Nashville said little and were not optimistic, and he did continue on to Kentucky. Back at Woodlands Margaret found that in James she had an invalid about the house.

Although she devoted most of her time to him and to the children, letters and plans flew between her and Sloan. On her early spring (1851) trip to Philadelphia, Margaret had found the plans to her liking. She now wrote Sloan:

> *They show exactly what I have in mind. The wing over the kitchen is an inspiration, for I can not bear to have them [the children] underfoot all day. It is, as is usual of late, a sad time for us. I must neglect everything and wait for Aunt B. to bring Mr. W's body back to Lexington. I still insist that we should be planted where we fall —these funeral journeys are becoming great and foolish trials.*

While in Lexington, she saw Dr. Benjamin Winslow Dudley and met his son, Charles Wilkins. She discussed James's health and Dr. Dudley encouraged her to make James either see some of the country's finest doctors in New Orleans or stay in Lexington where he could personally keep an eye on him. (Dr. Dudley, Sr., was one of the few medical men for whom James had any respect.)

Yet when Margaret returned, James still remained listless and detached. She must have detected something slowly moving away from her and while she tried to concentrate on every aspect of plans for the proposed building and watch over the constantly changing problems of her children, she was watching James.

> *There seems little of the old vitality . . . he is no longer the old James. The children have caught on to this obvious apathy. Lillie asked me if her father was ill. I tried to give her a light answer, but there is little use in this—she knows.*

Later she comments: "When Henry [Clay Erwin] comes I shall be able to talk with him about his father; he was the bulwark when the Prentiss affair was at its height." Years before, in New Orleans, James had been falsely accused of fraud, and Seargent Prentiss, orator and politician, had been the prosecutor. Prentiss had called James (among other things), "a coward . . . a disreputable character . . . without one redeeming virtue." He was later to retract this, saying that he had "traveled out of the record in the use of the offensive expressions."

James had come out unscarred and amused about the whole matter. But young Henry, age twenty-two, had taken offense at the old man's attack on his father and challenged him to a duel. The repeated assignations and postponements (because of Prentiss' age and failing health) became so tiresome to the New Orleans community that the matter dwindled, at last, into silence. James forgot, and this was unusual, for forgiving and forgetting did not run in the family.

This had been proven time and again. One famous example was that in 1807 when Charles Dickinson, the husband of James's cousin, Jane Erwin, was killed by Andrew Jackson in a duel.[10] Jane's father, Joseph Erwin, had already had considerable entanglements over lands, horse racing, and other matters (he is reported to have "done" Jackson out of 20,000 acres of land). Dickinson, young, loud-mouthed, bigoted, and usually in a state of drunkenness by sundown, had slandered Rachel Jackson one evening in a tavern. In themselves, words concerning the Jacksons were not patent matters, for they were the subject of much (local) scandal. Jackson, hearing of Dickinson's libelous assertions (regarding Rachel's not having secured a divorce before remarrying) in a public house, challenged him to a duel. This took place on the bank of the Red River early

10. The story of the duel is well told in many histories, the most colorful, perhaps, in Harnett T. Kane's *Gentlemen, Swords and Pistols* (New York: William Morrow, 1951), 50–52.

one April morning. Dickinson was fatally wounded and Jackson escaped with a grazed rib.

In this, the Erwin clan stuck together. Combined with past differences, the whole affair grew into a complex feud, not quieted by the editorials in the Erwin-controlled newspapers. Yet Henry Clay had sided with Jackson on political matters and was a friend; Richard Mentor Johnson also was close to both the Erwins and Jacksons. But the matter smoldered, for James's brother, John Patton Erwin, was editor and publisher of the then powerful Nashville *Banner and Whig* (for a time later he became postmaster of Nashville, then mayor and for the rest of his life an alderman of the city). As a writer, he had a habit of reporting matters precisely as they happened. This stolid, unblinking approach to the matted problems of the day did not keep him out of conflict with either citizenry or government. So, the local feud and its outcome was excellent fuel.

The inner family complications must have been fearful; there are supposedly no loyalties like those of the Old South. Family was family; friends were friends; everyone else and everything else, including, at times, the law, were strangers at best. John Patton had a record of winning. In all of his jobs he had formidable opponents; he had won out in an earlier scuffle with "Old Sam" Houston, an ally of Jackson's. So, in view of the Dickinson-Jackson duel, all the factions remained on the ready for almost fifty years, neither giving an inch.

Margaret was fond of the Erwins in Nashville, even before she became a close member of the family by her marriage to James. On her way from New Orleans to Lexington she often diverted her course of travel with or without James and stopped off in Tennessee to visit.

Although James was ill, Christmas 1850 must have been a happy one for the Erwins at Woodlands. All close connections had escaped the summer and fall epidemic of yellow fever. There was much to be thankful for that year. Yet Margaret missed her old admirers: Uncle Richard, who had died within the year, and Clay and Webster, both of whom were ailing and struggling with the country's desperate affairs in Washington. She was never diverted from her memories of the early years of association with them, although in their last years her path seldom crossed theirs, for she loathed Washington.

[To Carrie], December 1850, from New Orleans

> *I think of them perhaps every day of my life. And their distance or loss makes me see how little we have left, or will have left in the way of men—real men. I met a relative of that Mrs. Stowe's, a Miss Ophelia, who seems to be scouting like an Indian with her ear to the ground, just to uncover trouble. UTC [Uncle Tom's Cabin] is the WORST piece of ENDLESS misrepresentation that I have ever read. It is good to know that at least the plans for the house are here—I have the elevations and plans before me and I grow quite excited when I think that it is becoming an actuality. Soon I shall go back to the Lake.*

She did. But five years were to pass before the excavations for Mount Holly were begun.

Henry Johnson tried to persuade Margaret that it was too much of an undertaking, what with the illness of James and the country seething with a quite visible unrest; he thought the house plans too "grandiose." Others were dubious, but wisely kept their opinions to themselves. Matt[11] was "very smug about it all when I mistakenly opened the subject when he was present

---

11. Margaret was the third of eleven children and Matthew was the tenth. Therefore there is some mystery regarding the antagonism between two siblings of considerably different ages. The Matt referred to throughout her letterss must be her brother Matthew Johnson, of Chatham, Mississippi. Or could it be that an elder brother had the same middle name (something not unheard of in this particular period)? Yet certain later accounts of Matt's outlook and disposition are in keeping with Margaret's picture of him.

—and his 'friend' Mr. Douglas tried to get in on the matter—but I put an end to THAT. That little piglet!"

Early in January, 1851, Margaret was back in Lexington with some of the children and a governess. The old shadow was there. Everywhere she went Henry Clay seemed to be present. To Eleanor she wrote: "I feel like a ship without a rudder. I won't go to Ashland."

Her feelings were reflected in the opinion of many—that the most important man to gauge the temper of the country would not be around much longer. And the temperature was steadily rising. Clay would not be just a personal loss, or Kentucky's loss, but the nation would be deprived of one of the last great men of the period who had no ulterior dreams or motives. Clay and Webster (both were to die in 1852) had foreseen what could not long be held in check and, being powerless against the menace to so young a country, had felt a shadowing fear and sorrow for what they felt must come.

To Carrie, [early spring] 1851, from Lexington

My youngest, William, has been in a helpless state of sickness for three weeks. The doctors have few answers. They look as blank as hoot owls with their eyes closed. I have slept little and looked after him myself; the servants—except Nettie—are of no help. James postponed his trip to New Orleans for several more weeks; he is still ill, himself, but does little mentioning of it. What I heard of him when he was last there was not satisfactory.

William recovered; he did not die until 1908, in Washington, D.C. Whether this remark about James was relative to his growing illness or to his extramarital sex life is hard to say. Certainly Margaret was unruffled by the facts of the latter by this time. It may be assumed that his health was interfering with his business or it could have been the combination of business and Rachel.

To Samuel Sloan, March 2, 1851, from Lexington

I have not written for James looks like a ghost—he is not his old self. I do not think he will return to New Orleans for several months. We are quite concerned.

To Carrie, March 17, 1851, from Princeton, Mississippi

Perhaps I AM getting old and cantankerous and I am sure that my friends think so; my family KNOW it. With many worries here I have grown quite moody and irritable; and I dwell on unfortunate events and encounters of the past too much for anyone's good. My last trip to New York, what with all the pleasures of my shopping spree at Stewart's and Tiffany's, and seeing all my old friends, I was greatly put out by that Stowe woman—having to sit and listen to her air her views about matters of which she knows nothing, nothing at all.

I do not think I wrote you, as I was too angry to hold pen in hand; it was at Elsie's and SHE cornered me knowing I was southern. But I think she met her match and was completely astounded when I agreed with her on the slave question. She was somewhat set back when I told her that I think the question is only made worse by the meddling on the part of busybodies. H.S. was quite cool for the rest of the afternoon and I am afraid I may have embarrassed Mrs. Spangler, among others who were present. I think, most of them knowing my firmness and directness, they expected me to pull a gun from my reticule and shoot that jenny.

A great authoress HBS is not. The writing is jejune, sentimental, and piffling—and longer than the Bible. Well, what is done is done, and I regret none of it. I will say that the greater sympathies in the affair lay with me.

The meeting with Harriet Beecher Stowe was the third time that Margaret had come in contact with a person who would play a prominent role in the coming conflict. Her encounters with the future General Grant had been unpalatable; what she

had witnessed might have made even a weaker personality ac-
quire an immediate prejudice. Her attitudes toward abolition
never changed, but she was not one to admit it to her enemies
and detractors. She was later to free her slaves in 1858, knowing that the whole system was "rotten with faults and contained
wrongs within wrongs." Her friend, W. T. Sherman, was the
third actor.

Some unexplained sudden whim or necessity was responsible
for Margaret's making a trip to Philadelphia. As a result of some
uneasiness about her family, she wrote from there:

[To ?], 1851, from Philadelphia

> *I feel that I must go home once more and see my children, New
> Orleans, Lexington, Nashville, the Lake. Something tells me I
> should be there. Too, I hear that Uncle Henry is too concerned in
> Washington with irritating government matters and that his health
> is not at all good. But perhaps my anxiety is most of all concerned
> by my desire to see my own lands, complete my business with fa-
> ther, and see the Lake again—it is at its most beautiful and placid
> now and I am almost homesick just thinking and writing of it.
> Carrie has a beau! An Honourable at that ! They both seem
> smitten; such a match will flatten Philadelphia . . . Shall I ever
> see England again?*

She added:

> *Of course when I think of home it is of James that I think most, and
> about whom I am most worried.*

Two matters that she mentions have a hint of premonition in
them: her doubt about ever returning to England and her concern over James. He was only fifty-five but was still living his life
to the hilt, and was paying no attention to the doctors; they, on
their part, had never come to a conclusive diagnosis. James was
now suffering from a slight but seemingly chronic gastric disor-

der. His children numbered two by Rachel, six by Anne Clay and five by Margaret Johnson. It was at this time that he finally consented to selling the New Orleans house and ridding himself of Woodlands. The sale of the Kentucky house did not actually take place until after the death of Henry Clay in 1852 (it remained in the Clay family until 1864 or 1866). Margaret seemed somewhat relieved at the prospect of withdrawing from New Orleans. In a letter at about this time, she wrote to an unknown person:

> We shall bring the Pleyel piano from Magazine Street; but it is somewhat beyond human redemption and I don't think God is going to care much about infants squalling hymns —we have enough of that from the itinerant evangelists that descend on us only too often. To witness some of their meetings is enough to cure any would-be-saved souls and make them anxious for hellfire. I cannot stand by and be lectured on sins I did or did not commit (and possibly wanted to).

There is a gap of almost six weeks in extant letters. There is no trace of one to anyone. The next is to Carrie five weeks after James's death on June 1, 1851, in Lexington.

Although James had been ill for the previous two years, the situation never seemed precarious. Therefore, it was a terrible shock to Margaret when he died in Kentucky and she, not suspecting the seriousness of his illness, was in Mississippi.

Mount Holly   Built for Margaret Johnson Erwin; completed in 1859

Mount Holly, from the north—"the house is rather dragon-like and drawn-out."

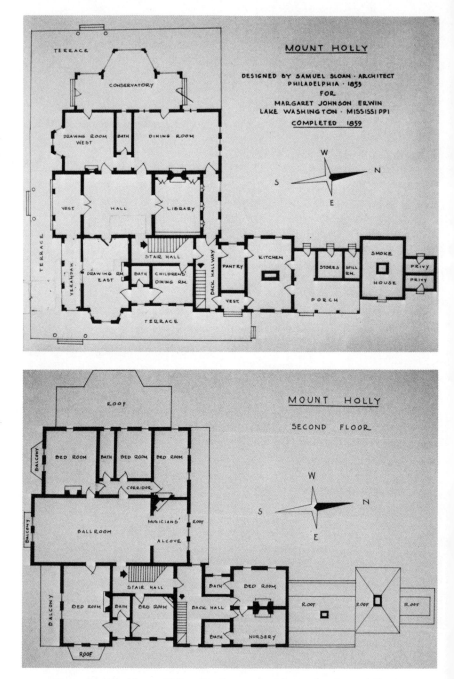

Floor plans for Mount Holly   By Stewart R. James, after Samuel Sloan

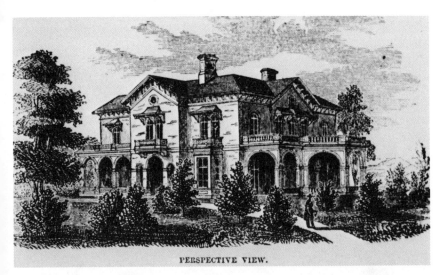

PERSPECTIVE VIEW.

Design No. 32, Calvert Vaux, "Perspective View"   Courtesy Dover Publishing Company

"There is a cheap quality to all the unnecessary details in most of his houses; there is as much resemblance to 'Italian Villas' in his work as there is in matching me to a cooter."

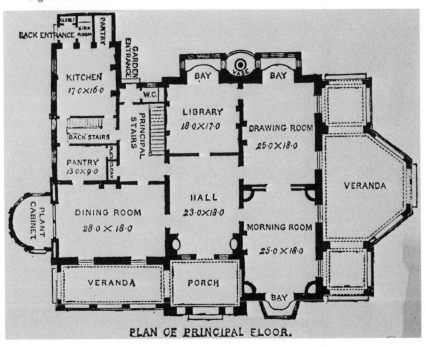

PLAN OF PRINCIPAL FLOOR.

Calvert Vaux: plan for an irregular villa, No. 32, in *Catalogue of Cottages and Villas*
Courtesy Dover Publishing Company

Original drawing by Samuel Sloan, architect, of Longwood
Built for Dr. Haller Nutt of Natchez, Mississippi

Courtesy Isabelle Ward Pollard

"I hear many things have gone wrong with Dr. Nutt's plans
for his extraordinary mansion in Natchez."

Richard Mentor Johnson   Courtesy Prints Division, New York Public Library

"Uncle Richard introduced the most *colorful* and jolly episode
into this staid family since the serpent prodded Eve."

Henry Clay, by Shobal Vail Clevenger

"In HC we possessed a truly acute man, a lovable man
. . . people have been blind to his greatness."

Ashland, Lexington, Kentucky   Home of Henry Clay:
1855 reconstruction, after the original

Louis Moreau Gottschalk   Courtesy Print Division, New York Public Library
"I have been to a concert by Louis M. G., a magnificent pianist and a great friend."

Mrs. Sallie Ward Hunt Armstrong Downs (1860)

". . . my cousin Sallie Ward. Her portrait by Healy is very pretty. But it seems to simper."

Julia Elizabeth Erwin, known throughout her life as "Lillie"
Portrait by John Pope, 1861, at Mount Holly
"The artist recommended by Mr. Sloan . . . quite outdid
himself in the portrait of Lillie."

Baroness Micaëla Almonester de Pontalba

Pontalba Collection of Louisiana State Museum

"James brought the B. de P. by to see the winter gardens. She was much impressed; even as I for her plans for the square in front of the cathedral."

Junius R. Ward 1850   Mrs. Junius R. Ward
                                  (née Martha Viley) 1851

Elizabeth Ward McGehee

"Junius and Matilda Ward's Elizabeth much
seen about with the ugliest young man I ever
laid eyes on." The young man in question,
George McGehee, became "Betty" Ward's
husband.

William Tecumseh Sherman
Engraved by Kellogg and Co. after a photograph

"He has never failed as a friend and *may* be the
reason for our complete isolation from the reali-
ties of the day."

John Cabell Breckinridge
"Cousin John B., I fear, is something
of a lightweight."

PART III

1851–1863

To Carrie, August 1851, from Lexington

To think that I was not there with him! I had been assured by Dr. Ben [Dudley] that there was no cause for alarm. I am only consoled by knowing that the entire family were with him. His interment was quite ceremonious and I have received many letters from prominent persons (I might add from some people he abhorred).

Yet nothing seems to have meaning now. I feel that I failed James, failed his children and our children, and that I am of no use to them or to myself. Guilt is an irrepressible, unanswerable condition when it separates the living from the dead.

James was buried near Anne . . . But wherever he is I feel that I must get on with my life, if not for myself, then for all our children. For Johnson is just a little over a year old and the girls are growing fast and need so much of my attention. Perhaps it is farewell to Europe and my friends there, for I should fear so for those I leave on this side. Dear, come to me when you can.

To Carrie, August 1851, from Nashville, Tennessee

I so deeply appreciated your dear letters and everyone has been so kind. The loss of James has been desolating, and all who know

*him must share this feeling. Eugene, particularly, seems most
affected.*

*I have letters from the Clays, of course, and Mr. Polk, Eleanor
and Mr. Sherman, Mr. Farman, Mrs. Beekman, and cousin
John B[reckinridge].*

*And I was deeply touched by a letter from Rachel (whom I
suppose I should resent in the manner of the "wronged wife," but
not at all). I feel quite concerned for her and hope that James pro-
vided for her and the children—so far I do not know; I shall try to
find out and if not successful in some way, I shall do so myself. Yet
I can not think of James as unthinking and careless in any relationship. Young HCE [Henry Clay Erwin] was the one upon whom I
leaned heaviest, I fear . . . a dear, dear man.*

*So James is at last in Lexington; at least now I know where he
is—no more of the expectancy of his arrival, the long nights of
waiting, the fears for his safety. The days of his travels between the
east and Kentucky and Tennessee, Mississippi and New Orleans
are over. When I go back to Lake Washington I must continue
what I have started; that house must be for all our children together. I have little heart for going on with the building, but so
much has gone into its planning, and so much depends on its completion.*

*Also, I would not want to give father or Matt the satisfaction of
seeing me desert what they so long have opposed. Speaking of Matt
–I had a very lugubrious missive from his appalling friend Mr.
Douglas. I suppose I shall have to acknowledge it—but each stab
of pen to paper will be most personal.*

Margaret's relations with her father, her brother Matt, and
some other members of her family were not totally oblique and
cold. Her intimates on the Lake seem to have been the McCaleb
family and the Turnbulls, Maria (Mary ?) particularly. In New
Orleans, she had close friends, among whom were the Bourges,
the Pelletiers, the Pontalbas, the de Generallys, and in Nash-

ville and in Kentucky, they were countless. She was, of course, devoted to Eleanor and William T. Sherman. There are no allusions to Sherman in any of her letters that are not of an open and complimentary nature.

To Carrie, October 1851

> *I don't know what humanity is coming to nor do I really care, I suppose. I have just heard more details of the Astor Place affair [the riots in New York City] two years ago when the burning of that handsome opera house took place. And all over two men I would not let [hand?] me from my carriage. When I saw them in their feeble vehicles I thought that the only more pompous and overrated actor than Macready was Edwin Forrest. What grunting and moaning! And the one is rather shapeless, as men go.*

William Charles Macready, the English tragedian, was playing *Macbeth* in the Astor Place Opera house in 1849. His American rival, Edwin Forrest, was acting in another play in the same vicinity. A mob, filled with anti-British feeling and class dissatisfaction and hatred, began a pro-Forrest riot that, in spite of the police and eventually the militia being called in, resulted in the death of twenty people and and injury to many more.

The Astor Place Riots, and the fact that people had been killed for reasons inane to her, was a part of the American scene. The reasoning, or lack of it, behind such events outraged her far more than the results. This all culminated after the gradual build-up of the hurrah of abolition, and the senselessness of secession. To her, the whole matter that resulted in the 1861–1865 conflict was a personal affront and a stab at both her broadmindedness and security. Yet, for some time, both survived.

The house in New Orleans was finally sold. (Late 1851?) To Eleanor she wrote:

> *After an absolutely useless trip to New Orleans, I found everything I had to do could have been done in two days—or without*

my presence at all. The house had been closed for so long that it took three days to air, and it still reminds me of a burial vault. I refrain from too many comments to the children, as the place was dear Anne's, and it must have held a world of memories for Henry and Eugene as well as for the other children who were old enough to remember. While in New Orleans this trip I met several more quite cultured and literate families; one, of course, I had known well—the Bourges. She is a good musician (a bit loud) but we can converse in French, which, to me, is always a great joy.

A further commentary:

Several of our relatives have now settled near Greenville (Mississippi), some miles above the Lake; it may turn out to be a pretty town, even if a flat one.

To Carrie, 1852, from Lexington

. . . so much difference in temperament and heredity—and the Germans have never learned the difference in pomposity and elegance; the French, although charming, have never clearly differentiated between elegance and superciliousness. The last, of which we, as a people, have gained so little from them [of their good qualities] that it puts us beyond the pale of criticism. It is only the English, with the muddle of their ancestry, who have combined and made for all a place of their own . . . elegant and articulate (when they wish to be), generous, wise, with impeccable manners.

When Margaret was on the Lake she was never quite comfortable in her father's or either of her brothers' houses. Kentucky was still home and it was closer to Louisville, Philadelphia, and New York, the cities in which she found the most diversion. Margaret wrote about Mount Holly to an otherwise unidentified "Martha." This is one of only two letters to Martha, which were furnished by Isabelle Ward Pollard, a cousin. There was no envelope, but it is reasonable to surmise that she was either Martha Viley of Kentucky or Martha Ward of Mississippi; both were Margaret's cousins:

To Martha, May 6, 1852

> I rode all the way to Mount Holly Plantation, one of father's properties here. The spring is lovely —but autumn is our most beautiful season, although it is more sorrowful than spring. Today I went through the woods to the lake and found the cabin (it is little more than that) belonging to Tom [?]. It is built on the exact spot that I should some day love to have a house; the surrounding forest is deep and beautiful and slumbering. With some of the lesser growth removed the view of the lake would be superb. Nettie was with me, afraid of her shadow, as usual. We came too near the nest of an eagle and one of the great birds swooped down; I thought Nettie would drop dead.

Undated, except for 1852 and obviously after midsummer, Margaret wrote:

> So good to be here again, surrounded by music and intelligence. Elizabeth Cary, Mrs. Louis Agassiz, whom I met long ago, was so happy to see me although we disagree on the Stowe woman. Mr. Strong showed me around the [Columbia] College where he may yet hold some position of great importance. Much talk at gatherings about the Morgan Selden affair [W. R. Morgan was a distant relative of Lillie's husband-to-be, Oliver Morgan]. This season, society in New York has had several bones to gnaw in the matter of William R. Morgan and his wife, Louise Selden. An emotionally unstable man, Morgan is accused of wife beating. It amounted to a battle royal —all quite scandalous. Then Charles Astor Bristed and his mistress met his wife in public and the two elegant women flew at each other like two mad hens, feathers flying. All this in Paris.
>
> So many people speak to me of Uncle Henry and what his loss means to the country. I went up to West Point, overnight, and

*saw the Noyes again, but traveling is beginning to make me quite
ill at ease—so* MANY *accidents—the* Henry Clay *near Yonkers,
and a little later, the* Reindeer, *both crowded in midsummer.*
[*Both ships met tragic accidents on the Hudson in mid-1852, with
many deaths.*] *I met the Abbott Lawrences,* [1] *but I did not reveal
to them my relationship to Sallie Ward. My dear Daniel Webster
very ill* [*he died October 24*].

Margaret must have stayed in New York for some weeks this
time, for she mentions attending William Makepeace Thackeray's lecture: "A most amusing evening; I am sure that *he* can be
quite vicious if the notion takes him."

Undated, with no place name, this letter had to follow the
preceding letter and it well may have also been written from
New York soon after Webster's death.

To Carrie

*Uncle Richard, Uncle Henry and Mister Webster, all gone!
We are deluding ourselves if we think that we have any real men
left. I feel that most of the people I have really loved are deserting
me. It is hard to imagine this country without a Clay or a Webster
—their common sense and uncommon rhetoric were unmatched
and, unlike so many of their fellows, you could not only understand them but believe them. A dear letter from Mary [Todd] with
a postscript from Mr. Lincoln deploring the loss of these great
men. So many of these we have are like volcanoes, spouting ashes.
In HC we possessed a truly acute man, a lovable man. But tragedy struck him once too often, and the people have been blind to
his greatness; his failure to attain the ascendant position was almost the last thing that he could bear—first broken by Anne's
death then by Henry Jr.'s, and the tragedies of the other children.
Yet James and I always seemed to make up much to him and I have*

1. Abbott Lawrence, merchant and politician, was United States representative in
Congress (1834–1836; 1838–1840) and U.S. minister to Great Britain (1849–1852).
He was the father-in-law of Margaret's cousin, Sallie Ward.

been with all the children at Woodlands *as much as it has been possible for me to do so. No, no,* God *is not* always *wise.*

I can not ever forget that it was he [Clay] *who insisted on my earliest travels in England and France, and he contributed so much in the way of beautiful things, both circumstances quite beyond my capacities for decision. I suppose I must* dream *of spring in England and be done with it. What fools, what frivilous thoughtless fools we were to leave, and cut ourselves loose from a country of* human beings *for what is fast becoming a cauldron of knaves.*

And more to Carrie, still undated, and incomplete:

For all Miss Beam's faults—and we were very young and probably had more than she—she was an old dear. I can not forget that she almost turned green at the sight of a goblet of water, remembering the voyage.

The deaths of Clay and Webster really made 1852 a tragic year for Margaret. In another comment, she wrote:

I feel all the great and good are leaving us to the grafters and swindlers . . . only out of what is now a void may come someone of great worth—perhaps Mary's husband [Abraham Lincoln].

Again in New York, in the spring of 1853: "We heard Alboni in *La Sonambula* and *Gazza Ladra*; a large voice, whatever else."

To Carrie, May 10, 1853, from New York

What a grim accident on the New Haven RR! So stupid! An open drawbridge flung one car carrying more than fifty people into the Norwalk River. All caused by the carelessness of an engineer who had been dismissed two years before, then rehired by an equally guilty board of directors. Another "investigation" begun. We will not hear of it again.

By 1853, the plans for Mount Holly were complete with the exception of certain details (constantly changing as Margaret had some new thought concerning them). In a letter from New Orleans that year she says, "My thanks to Mr. Vaux for his welcome suggestions."

This is one of only a few instances in her (discovered) letters that the name of Vaux was mentioned. He was Calvert Vaux, architect and landscape architect, who, with Frederick Law Olmstead ("bombastic and expostulating on subjects of which he has little knowledge"), designed Central Park in New York City.

Confounding the matter of the identity of Mount Holly's architect, *Harper's New Weekly* from November, 1855, shows Vaux's plan for and a sketch of the facade of a house almost identical to Mount Holly except that the Vaux plan, for an "Irregular Villa,"—design No. 32 from his *Catalogue of Cottages and Villas*—is in complete reverse and on a smaller scale. Vaux had been a pupil of William Strickland, as Sloan had been.

Whether Mount Holly was an adaptation by Sloan from Vaux or whether the latter's design, of a date three years later, was an adaptation of Sloan's work, remains an unanswered, perhaps never to be answered, question. The Vaux catalogue item remains unimportant in itself, for the letters show that Margaret had her plans by 1853 and that Sloan or one of his men superintended, from time to time, the building of Mount Holly from 1856 onward. J. E. Edmonds in his *Lake Washington* (1899) says "Henry Johnson's daughter, Margaret, purchased Mount Holly Plantation from her father and by 1859 had completed building one of the most unique mansions of the section with the help of a famed Philadelphia architect." This somewhat narrows the origin, since Vaux was not known as a Philadelphia architect; he was English, and a protégé of horticulturist and architect Andrew Jackson Downing, and later an associate of Frederick Law Olmstead. General Edmonds, of Asheville, N.C., was a close friend and frequent hunting companion of the Johnsons, Erwins, Princes, Footes, and Worthingtons. His excellent memory remained with him for half a century after this was written, and until his recent death.

To Carrie, May 27, 1853, from Princeton, Mississippi

A loud and prolonged argument with father and Matt. Did not believe half of what either of them said regarding the river and the danger of the city [New Orleans], and there seems another invasion of fever [yellow] there . . . a season of pestilence.

The year ended on an even grimmer note, for by December cholera was decimating the population of New Orleans and there were scattered cases throughout the East. In the same letter:

Looking at the stubbornness and narrowness and lack of feeling in these two [Matt and Henry] I sometimes wonder if I —and others of my generation—am not the result of some nocturnal dallying on the part of mother. I hardly dare hope.

And later yet, same letter:

I must approach father on closing my deal with him regarding the plantation. He MUST *see my need, with all the little ones about. I can not have them scattered from Lexington to New Orleans all year like orphans.*

On June 6 she wrote:

Three friends have died and I have a feeling that New Orleans is not the place for me to be just now. I must go back to the Lake.

It turned out to be a wise decision, for the plague swept the city that summer and over ten thousand people died of it. At one time, during August, it is reported that a death occurred every five minutes. But with cooler weather the sickness abated.

Margaret made another trip north and after a brief stay in New York she stopped in Philadelphia, where she saw a model for her house and was "pleased" besides having "many happy hours with Carrie." She returned by way of Lexington and Louisville, and from there traveled down the river to Princeton. But before leaving New York she wrote: "I hear the Morgan scandal has at last been approached in the paper; it is just about time someone put an end to that ugly beast."

Quite aside from avoiding the crowds of the 1853 exhibition in New York City, Margaret seems to have had a gay time of it.

> For all the troubles of cousin Sally with Bigelow Lawrence, I find I am more impressed with the Lawrences than any New Englanders I have ever been subjected to—they are really quite intelligent and natural people; through them I have met the Schermerhorns and John Astor. The latter, rather listless—probably fatigue from the "counting house."

A further comment on cousin Sallie appears in a letter dated July 7 (probably of 1854):

> Whenever I am in this city now the more I hear of Sallie W. She is giving the natives a taste of the grandiose. An enormous house and dinners for fifty, with music by the opera orchestra. What a performance! I am not sure that Dr. John applauds but he seems smitten. She is quite pretty but her performance is questionable. Granted she had been and done and seen just about everything . . . but I have a feeling she is in for a fall comparable to Eve's.

About a year after Sallie Ward's divorce from Bigelow Lawrence, she had married a prominent Louisville physician, Dr. Robert P. Hunt. They moved to New Orleans, where Sallie's father, Robert Johnson Ward, had amassed much of his wealth, and where Dr. Hunt was well known. Her entrance into New Orleans society was without effort. But Margaret was wrong about such a fall. Sallie outlived three of four husbands. With her fortune, jewels, and social standing intact, she lived on in the Galt House in Louisville, dying there in 1896.

The Crimean War definitely put an end to any projected visit by Margaret to France and Italy, as she remarks upon in a letter to Eleanor.

To Eleanor, June 1854, from Lexington

> *England and France at war with Russia; they are as entangled in mistakes of their own making as we—what fools!*

Meanwhile Margaret settled on the location for her house.

To Eleanor, December 31, 1854, from Princeton, Mississippi

> *As I have just written your husband, I have completed my arrangement with father—*the plantation is now mine! *The plantation and the beautiful Lake property where I shall begin to build. The price seemed unreasonable but I did not quarrel, as I can afford it. Thos.* [Redd] *is acting as "trustee," as father does not believe a woman capable of anything beyond tatting and having children—he must be taught. Matt takes the same attitude.*
>
> *You must see our Lake again—at all seasons it is too beautiful, but it is in the quiet of mid-summer and endless twilights that I like it best. But then—with a typical woman's mind—there is spring, and later the* tristesse *of our falls (or are all autumns filled with unreasonable nostalgia?)*

On the same day she wrote to Carrie:

> *The deed is done (an unintended pun)! Father and Mother put their names to the* voluminous *paper, with cousin Thos. as "trustee" today! Now I have my plantation and Mr. Miller and Thos. to advise me. I feel by this act of independence I am making the first step towards freeing myself of a most cloying family relationship—and there is another development which I shall surprise you with in a few days! Or it may be a week or two—just a thing I will not tell until it is a* fait accompli . . . *for the family will bay like hounds, except Lou, Em, Mary Bell, and Claude (who cares for*

little on this earth, anyway, outside of his own comfort). You must come down when Mr. Sloan does.

To Carrie, January 25, 1855, from Lexington

Early in December I wrote you of my thoughts on a second marriage. [That letter is missing; this one is the first clue regarding its contents.] In spite of my misgivings and much Johnson criticism, I married Dr. Charles Wilkins Dudley, Dr. Ben's son, on January 14. I am most content with my decision and believe that we shall be quite happy. No one will ever occupy the place of James — his personality is not often equalled. I hope it will not give you apoplexy when I say that being married to a Casanova — and that he was — is not without its daily doubts and excitements.

I only hope that all the children will accept Dr. Dudley; most of them know him and the Dudleys are greatly admired by the Clay family. For his part, he seems quite willing to leave Kentucky for permanent residence on Lake Washington.

Not to confuse you, this was the matter I barely hinted upon in my letter of three weeks ago. I was right: father and mother and Matt were outraged. So soon after James . . . You can guess the rest. But the days do, indeed, go by so quickly, and I must be prepared for any event in these changing times.

To Carrie, from New Orleans

I saw Cousin Sallie at another of her soirees. I think no empress of our time ever puts on as many jewels — or as many airs. But the evening was made worth my time by meeting Adelina Patti there; she and Sallie seem to know each other well.

While our days here were elegant and a carry-over from the great days of H.C. and Anne, our balls were simple teas compared to these affairs. R.H. seemed pale and dejected. I feel no jealousy; Sallie is not beautiful — but she is radiant!

To Eleanor, January 17, 1855, from Lake Washington

Although the negotiations are over I feel that the price I have paid for Mount Holly was not quite fair and I wish William [Sherman] to know this. I hear that John Randolph bought a place in Louisiana for about one third of what I paid father—with far less cash involved. Yet, as William knows, I can afford it and I refuse to be troubled by a small thing like money. But to feel that one's own kin has acted in an almost dishonest manner—need I say more?

I have great plans for my acquisition and I hope to get to them soon. There is so much to be done here and Mr. Sloan has gone to such pains to please me.

I wrote you of my marriage and I have no misgivings about this step. Although my relatives are treating me as if I had escaped from a nunnery and gone into a brothel.

Dr. Dudley was evidently more than ready to leave Kentucky to settle in Mississippi. Margaret Erwin was a wealthy woman, for besides what was her own, she inherited all James's properties in Louisiana, Arkansas, Tennessee, and Pennsylvania.

To Carrie

I am very disturbed over conditions in New York and generally in the north and east. We have our problems here but I think they can be resolved without the mealy-mouthing of know-nothings and do-gooders. Most of the harm in this world is done by people with "good intentions"—or perhaps with misguided (and, often, depraved) intentions.

It was dear H.C. [Henry Clay] who first advised us to travel under a nom de plume. It was quite wise for, looking back, some of the ships and other conveyances we trusted were far from innocent in regard to the human element, had they known who we were, what our reticules actually held, or what little importance we did (or did not) assume. I am but a wary believer in God's eye being on the sparrow, et cetera. I have seen too much of vanity and

avarice and deluded humanity to believe that Anyone has their
omnipotent eyes walling around on each and every one of us.
Johnson has been dragging around for a week. Listlessly. He
has been seen by a doctor and there is nothing obvious wrong. But
it is hard to get common, mule sense out of a five year old. I am not
indifferent to my children and their needs—indeed, I think I am
too much upon them. But I cannot stand mysteries and any such
thing had better come out or be gone.

Many hours of research have not uncovered what *nom de*
plume Margaret and Carrie used in their travels. Perhaps it
changed from trip to trip. Passenger lists from transatlantic ships
of the time have been consulted; hotel registers would probably
offer the same negative results. Not of great import, of course,
but it would still be interesting to know whether Margaret's
humor or wisdom was apparent in her assumed name(s).

[To ?], March 1855, from Chatham, Mississippi

Again we are inundated by that miserable, filthy river. The
County Seat is in a precarious state and I should not be surprised
to hear of it going at any time. Too, Cousin J[unius] W[ard] (who
is just completing his great TEMPLE *in Kentucky)* [2] *is worried sick*
over the large house he has begun at the Landing—for it is even
closer to the river. I shall—for once—remain silent, but I thought
he was a fool from the beginning. The lands in the vicinity of the
Lake are not only safer but far more beautiful. Yet the Wards have
always considered gambling and unique gestures a virtue. I do not.

As had become usual, her intuition proved correct: Princeton, the Washington County seat, was mostly destroyed that
summer by the flooding river; what was left was finished off in

---

2. Ward Hall was completed for Junius R. Ward in 1853. Overall it has been considered one of the best examples of Greek Revival of the "immediately pre-war years,"
with "palatial formality and magnificence." Only the house remains—the original barns,
stables, and outbuildings, including extensive greenhouses, have long since vanished.

the following year. With the courthouse and its many records went the Georgian-Palladian mansion that had already cost Junius Ward $30,000. When not in Kentucky, the Wards lived in a frame farmhouse, Fair Oaks (now Erwin), the Ward's "east" plantation. This was later, in 1881, to be the residence of Margaret Erwin's son, Johnson, after his marriage to Matilda Ward.

Yellow fever had become a thing to be most feared, for each year some family suffered a loss. Even if one recovered, it was a most disabling complaint, the effects lasting sometimes for months.

To Samuel Sloan, July 12, 1855, from Lake Washington

> I regret that you have been unable to come to us during the early summer—but the flooding has been deplorable. And it is probably as well for your sake as the fever has taken a great toll once more. I know of few families that have not been touched by it.

To Samuel Sloan, July 20, 1855, from Lake Washington

> I have now decided to go ahead—finally, definitely—with the exact plans that we made in 1853 [?] for the house on Lake Washington. I have made further arrangements for buying [more] land adjoining Mount Holly Plantation, with my father, Henry Johnson, and with Junius Ward (on the west). I visualize the house facing the Lake, southwest; there lies my whole lakefront property.
>
> I would like to take advantage of this prospect, a most beautiful one at any time of the year. In doing this I would like some changes made in the facade—a most imposing and unusual one, and with more than adequate fenestration and galleries in this direction. Last year we discussed mainly what I do not wish in my proposed house.

She failed to achieve her wish; the windows in Mount Holly, although "adequate," are tall and narrow.

To Carrie, August 10 [1855], from Lake Washington

I sometimes think the Wards, and Willa V. and my other
cousins, the Warfields, out of their minds. After all the success
with that horse, they sold out to Richard Ten Broeck—that scoun-
drel . . . they will live to see the day that horse is worth its weight
in gold.

We here have our interest in racing but it is far from the exciting
sport that it is in Kentucky. James with his knowledge would have
found it a poor thing, indeed. A race track some miles from Wade
H[ampton] is a sorry substitute. But then any innovation lightens
our ennui. No, I am never bored, but I do have memories and
longings that are not easily dismissed.

There is much that I re [torn off in the middle of this sentence].

The above letter refers to the racehorse Lexington (first named
Darley), which was bought for $5,000 by Richard Ten Broeck
from Junius and Robert Ward, Dr. Elisha Warfield, and Captain Willa Viley. Ten Broeck was something of a drifter and op-
portunist with interests in the New Orleans racing world. But
this transaction of his paid off well, with Warfield, Viley, and
the Wards losers, for Lexington became one of the most successful racers of his day. After seven spectacular races it was discovered that Lexington was losing his sight; he was put to stud,
having been sold to one Robert A. Alexander for the (then)
unheard of sum of $15,000. Because of the muddled records
created by the Civil War, the exact number of Lexington's offspring is not known; however, it has been said that he is the
ancestor of almost every American-bred winner of this century.

The Mississippi racetrack referred to was evidently the one
of which remnants remained in the early twentieth century. By
then it was on a plantation owned by the Harris-Dulaney family
and was seldom, if ever, put to its original use.

Sometime during the year she wrote once again to "Martha"
about Mount Holly.

To Martha, [1855], from Lake Washington

Almost before the ink was dry on the deed I had the shanty on Mount Holly leveled, and they are now making a larger clearing, preparing for the excavation of the house I hope to see there. I shall leave many of the great trees, but I wish large expanses of lawn between. Curiously there is almost a circle of large oaks surrounding the place where I wish my house to stand. Much to father's amusement I have given a name to each of them. Perhaps I should follow the lake shoreline and do the same for the amazing incomparable cypress; there are eagles' nests in two. I should love to see their young—but I value my life.

At certain times of the year the lake seems a sea of ducks and geese, having winged their way northward or southward according to the season; these must be protected, as must the flamingos that arrive for a brief stay in the first warm weather, all pink and white, and not too friendly with our blue herons.

Excavation for Mount Holly was not begun until the fall of 1855 so it is possible the above letter was written in the summer. Margaret was pregnant by the time autumn rolled around, she "thought"; a few weeks later it was a certainty.

To Samuel Sloan, October 1855, from Lake Washington

I shall be most anxious to see what magic you will produce in the slight changes I have suggested. You may send the plans, elevations, and drawings to my brother Matthew's at The Burn.

I appreciate your kindness on my last visit to Philadelphia. Please give my regards to Carrie.

Please do not repeat me, but Mr. Vaux's suggestions [?] will not do, after all—I like yours far better. There is a sameness, there is a cheap quality to all the unnecessary details in most of his houses; there is as much resemblance to "Italian Villas" in his work as there is in matching me to a "cooter" [the Negro's name for a turtle]. So I am leaving the matter entirely in your hands. I have seen the two Strickland houses and as beautiful as they are I do not wish, *as I said long ago, anything pertaining to the Greek, Roman, or Egyptian temple.*

Vaux did supposedly design one house, Ammadelle, in Oxford, Mississippi, that was an excellent example of the contemporary explosion of Italian architectural demand in America. Yet, regrettably, most of the Italian villa-derived houses of the period—including Mount Holly—lack the dignity and simplicity of what they were supposed to emulate. Mount Holly comes nearer than Ammadelle and certainly Vaux's Design No. 32, but it does miss the mark.

Mount Holly is in many ways a supposed replica of her uncle Victor Flournoy's home, Aldemar, which was located at Leota Landing—the house now swallowed up by the Mississippi. The Flournoy house had two wings extending toward its rear instead of the one that Mount Holly possesses. Was this Vaux or Sloan? It is probably another question that will never be answered, the building having gone the way of the uncompleted Ward mansion.

In the same letter to Sloan, Margaret fired a volley at another designer of her day:

> I hope I will not offend you when I say that my one meeting with F[redrick]L[aw]Olmstead left me with the impression of a pompous, know-nothing, loud bigot. We have them here, too. I would not let that man design a cabbage patch for me; Mr. Vaux seems little more than his sycophant and slave.

To Samuel Sloan, December 7, 1855, from Princeton, Mississippi

> The revised sketches and the proposals for the house are quite amazing. I see that you were most perceptive and intuitive as to my requirements and those of an already large (and still increasing!) family. There are a few points that are not quite clear, but I

*am sure that we can untangle them when I see you in the spring.
You will be most welcome and I am sure that you will agree with
me on the site I have selected for the house. It is by far the most
pleasing—in addition to having the most altitude (remember our
River!). Father may already regret his generosity.*

It is difficult to see any "generosity" in her father's gesture (nor
did Margaret in other letters commenting on the matter; see p.
77). Margaret bought the plantation for $100,000, an almost
fantastic amount of money in those days. Perhaps *generosity* is
used in sarcasm; or perhaps the site so delights her that it seems
no one would part with it for any price.

Continuing to Sloan, she wrote:

*On inspecting the elevations, I wonder if the roof is not a trifle
too low, giving the effect that the house is wearing a mashed, black
hat. [This inconsistency is, I suppose, typical, for later she "sug-
gests" that the roof be not "peaked" but almost flat.]. But this is a
small matter and I am sure you know best. The doorway is tres
formidable, but this, too, we can discuss. I especially admire
the unusual shape for the conservatory and the designs for the
chimneys.*

My kindest regards to your family.

To Carrie, January 10, 1856, from Princeton, Mississippi

*We are a family that always seems astride politics, like it or not.
I suppose one should be filled with pride that another member
might be* ANOTHER *Vice President. (I did not think that John
[Breckinridge] was made of the right material.)*

To Samuel Sloan, February 8, 1856, from Nashville, Tennessee

*Yours of the 23rd rec'd. The second revised version of the house
shows some afterthought on your part and I agree with you on
most details. I have no objection to the added cost of the two rooms*

for nurseries, nor of the terraces being extended in both width and length. The size of the smokehouse is rather extraordinary; do you think it being in such proximity—actually connected to the main house—creates any danger from fire?

You would have heard from me before this but I have had to be in Nashville due to an illness in the family. I shall go on to Louisville and then to Lexington where my child will be born later in the spring. In the meanwhile my sisters are keeping the family in hand on the Lake.

Margaret was next in New York. In a postscript to a letter from there: "Heinrich Heine is dead—in Paris—and he was buried in Pere Lachaise. A great and unhappy man."

[To Eleanor], February 25, 1856, from New York

I have been to a most impressive concert by Louis M[oreau] G[ottschalk], a magnificent pianist and a great friend; I was delighted that he played none of his own works. I have had dinner en seul with him twice, but he is very busy, more than fifty concerts here alone. [He gave eighty that season.]

Her next letter, also from New York, was dated April 15:

[To Carrie]

We saw a most amusing and droll play last week, London Assurance,[3] then to an elegant dinner.

To Samuel Sloan, May 1856, from Lexington

Have no fears regarding the chapel at the southern end of the Lake. Mr. Knox and Mr. T[urnbull?] have agreed with me that it shall go on as planned. It is not of my faith but that is of little consequence. Please let me have the remaining bills due and I will see that they are attended to at once. I deplore certain other members

3. Dion Boucicault's play *London Assurance* was revived with vast success in London in 1973 and there was a limited engagement in New York in late 1974.

of the congregation's change of mind and heart. Their attitude is very shallow, should I be asked; I have not been nor shall I be, no doubt. *The Bishop [Otey] is pleased with my decision. The lack of action on the part of the others —he will not make comment. Why are the clergy so indecisive? A small wonder that hell lurks just in reach.*

With every regard to you, Mrs. Sloan and Carrie,

To Eleanor, June 1856, from Lexington

. . . *it was all quite simple and little Charlie [Charles Wilkins Dudley, Jr., was born in May, 1856] seems a very good baby. Cousin John [Breckinridge] with Buchanan —it now seems it should be just the other way around, not that any of it matters too much, for the country is in a turmoil that will not end soon, no matter* WHO *supposedly leads us. All this talk of states gathering their militia, states' borders being overrun —it is the beginning of a rebellion that I feel will have no end.*

To Samuel Sloan, June 1856, from Lake Washington, Mississippi

I know that we are taking some chance of total loss and certainly procrastination in allowing the dining room and the two drawing room mantels to be done in Italy, but in both instances I am willing to gamble. The smaller marble pieces for the upstairs are quite satisfactory in design and can be carried out quite well in Philadelphia. The bricks for the ovens are as per your specifications and this material should be on hand during the next year, but pay no attention if my impatience makes itself visible.

. . . *what, even with the bare outlines, I am consulting with botanists and plain gardeners. I wish that Mr. V [Vaux?] might guide me in this, although I am sure that there are few who would allow me to have my way with my rose garden.*

[To ?], June 20, 1856, from "The Lake"

. . . *at least some good seems to emanate from New England.*

Bennett's Herald *is supporting the south by being firm on Frémont's stand for the Presidency.*

John Charles Frémont was nominated by the Republicans with a
highly idealistic and seemingly workable platform. Even though
defeated, he became something of a hero to many in both the
north and south (even though he was the new Republican party's
first national candidate).

In the letter above, Margaret also wrote, "I hear that the
J.Q.A. Ward base for the figure of Washington is magnificent
and the whole will be shown some time in July in New York."
This refers to the Henry Kirke Brown statue of George Washington that stands in Manhattan's Union Square. Margaret evidently thought that the statue itself was by Ward (an Urbana,
Ohio, relative of the Wards), not just the pedestal. The figure
of George Washington in front of the old Treasury Building in
New York's Wall Street *is* by Ward, as are several other statues
in the city.

To Samuel Sloan, August 11, 1856, from Lake Washington

   . . . *the design for the doorway of the house reminds me of the
Baths of Caracalla, and pleases me not one whit. It has overtones
of Vaux at his least sublime. I enclose a sketch more to my view of
what the entry should be; the single heavy arch could be left, with a
single, narrower one on each side of it. And the overdoor decoration should not be so heavy and just* hang. *Could it not be made
more delicate and the whole supported by four—or even six—
brackets of some sort?*

Unfortunately, the original design for the doorway has not
appeared, but Margaret's revision remains, both in her rough
sketch and in reality. The actual doorway shows that her judgment seems correct. Sloan, after this "set-to," must have been
made conscious once more of the will of the woman with whom
he was dealing, one whose ideas could not be ignored.

[To ?], September 20, 1856, from Lexington

I had made up my mind to forget that Stowe creature but became involved with her odious book, Dred: A Tale of the Great Dismal Swamp. *Indeed, the right woman writing at the right time on the right subject; indeed, it is a* DISMAL *book! She seems obliged by her very nature to consort with subjects quite above her head . . . too much hymn singing in that family. I see that vapid face on every page and shall not be able to finish it.*

[To ?], November 1856, from Lake Washington

John Floyd soon to be in Buchanan's cabinet, I think as Secretary of War. I shall be all for him if he can keep us away from it. Cousin John B[reckinridge], I fear, is something of a lightweight.

To Samuel Sloan, December 11, 1856, from Lake Washington

Your kindness touches me deeply. My recent stay in Philadelphia surpassed any previous one in enjoyment. The additional touches to my house delight me.

On returning here I found that much progress had been made on my "villa" (as Carrie WILL *call it!), but at this season the whole country where it will stand looks most dreary and barren in outline. [The foundation] looks unusually small. You will remember that Mr. Strickland warned me of this!*

If the war in Europe continues I suppose I shall have to forego any extensive tour, as planned, next year. [She did not go].

[To ?], February 1857, from Lake Washington

It is early for spring here and I am anxious to see the metamorphosis of my pile of bricks. I wanted the finished house to be a surprise and hope that it does not take place in our grim winters. Early spring here can be cold and windy, yet even Paris would win no decorations in that respect.

87

To Samuel Sloan, April 8, 1857, from Lake Washington

I attended the consecration of St. John's three days ago—in a snow storm (in April!!!) —and I wish to commend you on your part in it. It is a very handsome piece of ecclesiastical architecture, reminding me of some of the beautiful parish churches[4] in England. It is not pretentious in any way and it deserves the beautiful setting that Mr. McCaleb so generously gave it. After the ceremonies I had a talk with Wade [Jr. or Sr.?] Hampton, Mr. Chapman, and Mr. and Mrs. Smith. They are all most complimentary. The present organ, as yet, is shrill.

The church is a wonderful addition to our small community, and the grounds most peaceful for a cemetery.

To Samuel Sloan, August 1857, from Lake Washington

. . . whether the doors downstairs are to be painted or not is quite a question. If in oak, I see no reason why they should not be. But if they are in walnut, rosewood, or mahogany they would be too beautiful to be covered. The stair rail is inconsequential to me; any hardwood seems the best solution for I can not feature removing splinters from my children's derrieres every day in the week.

To Samuel Sloan, February 8, 1858, from Lake Washington

In addition to the iron work for the balconies, the two marble statues, and the three mantels, we still lack the glass for the "pantry porch" and the conservatory. I do not know what to think of this. I suppose I could obtain the glass from New Orleans. What shall I do? I want the conservatory! They can freeze in the pantry, for all I care, but I do want my plants to survive.

4. In a letter to Haller Nutt in Natchez, Mississippi, Samuel Sloan says: "If you meet with Bishop Polk say to him that I am now preparing several plans for the small churches about such as he named and will forward them in the course of a week or ten days." (Sloan to Nutt, July 16, 1860, in Sloan-Nutt Letters, Huntington Library, San Marino, California). Doubtless one of the churches referred to in this letter is St. John's.

To Samuel Sloan, March 20, 1858, from Lake Washington

I do not quite understand the matter of the water pressure to take care of the W.C.'s upstairs—perhaps you can elucidate? The house has now taken form and I could not be more pleased. The design for the brickwork of the chimneys is very handsome, indeed. The wrought iron is a long time in arriving—just the one balcony as yet. And still no glazing for the pantry and the conservatory. But I shall be patient, as I know that you have many other things with which to contend.

To Samuel Sloan, May 11, 1858, from Lake Washington

I am delighted that you could combine other business matters with your visit to the Lake, and arrange them so that you were here for the very first steps in construction . . . did you ever see as many bricks? A silly question, for of course you have . . . the children seem to think that they were made for them and have been responsible for some of the most ungodly structures . . .

To Samuel Sloan, May 16, 1858, from "The Lake"

I am quite certain that you know more of the structural necessities concerning the roof over the ballroom, but do consider that I do not want a "peaked" roof and that a flat roof with a shallow fake gable in front, if rightly angled or "raked," seems entirely adequate for this climate. After all, we have but little snow and the weight of it would never be a matter over which to be concerned with subsequent disaster. Were the house in Kentucky it would be a different matter.

To Carrie, July 4, 1858, from Lake Washington

The preoccupation of humanity with anniversaries leaves me somewhat rebellious . . . most of them are marred by great tragedy—preceding or following, it does not matter. The national setting aside of one date for celebration—pshaw, it is like saying that "on this day in 1810 great aunt Martha was so disturbed by wind on her stomach." And it means even less except for some already dilatory person being able to squander the public's time. I do not refer to Christmas or Easter, of course, but I feel that "saint's days" and observances for the birth of this or that political drone or political event are just so much rubbish.

To Samuel Sloan, July 1858, from "The Lake"

All seems to go well, but the wood railings look heavy and awkward. I hope I may receive the balance of the cast iron in the autumn.

The brick terrace turned out well, the way that I knew it would, from my observation of certain English houses. The well-drained space keeps out dry rot (our own southern brand) and the hordes of insects we must expect to contend with. The peacocks on it are most decorative, but their days are numbered. I will not be awakened before every dawn by their ungodly noise, which I am told will get worse as they grow older. So they will not grow much older, not with the holidays on the way.

I have been criticized for not insisting upon a more imposing stairway (the central one); I am quite satisfied with the hall as it is.

The labor imported for construction has worked out much to our mutual advantage. We have few here capable of doing more than burning bricks (or dinner, as it turned out last evening). The men you have sent down have been comfortably housed and I try to see that they are well fed and furnished some amusement. The Lake seems to afford them great pleasure.

[To ?], July 1858, from "The Lake"

The niches fascinate me and I am anxious to see them inhabited. The double doors to the library were the only solution to the entrance hall—a single door would merely appear as if it opened into a privy. I can only suppose that they will rarely be closed, anyway, what with my menage.

The "menage" at this point consisted of some of the Anne Clay–James Erwin children, all of the Margaret Johnson–James Erwin brood, and the single duckling, Charles Wilkins Dudley.

To Samuel Sloan, July 1858, from "The Lake"

> *The view of the house from the north is rather dragon-like and drawn-out. But I think that when the park is thinned out and then fully planted, and my walled garden outside the conservatory is finally done, one will not be so very conscious of so very* MUCH *house. For all that, I am in love with it already.*

To Samuel Sloan, August 1858, from "The Lake"

> *Mr. S. or one of his men will transfer the money from New York to your account. This, I believe, fulfills the contract as I remember it. Correct me if I am mistaken. The earlier ten thousand dollars merely represented my faith and assurance, and the expenses of your traveling was such a piddling amount we will not mention it. The present thirty eight thousand does not include the items which have been ordered for the completion of the house (the iron work and the statuary and glass). You will keep me appraised of what this will amount to and I will remit at once.*
>
> *I greatly admire your tenacity in seeing that all materials have so far got through; I am sure it has been no small feat. It has been most fascinating watching the building take shape and I am more than pleased. Again, the addition of the two large rooms in the nursery wing makes me extremely happy . . . cutting the children off with their own hall and stairs.*

Margaret constantly alluded to keeping the younger children apart from their older siblings and parents; a single notation gives a clue to her thinking: "The people of Greece and Rome and earlier civilizations were wise in not parading infants in front of their elders; what nonsense about Cornelia and her 'jewels'—bawling fakes, I will wager. There are few more exas-

perating things than the whining or prattling or aimless jump-
ing about on the part of children; there are friends I will not
visit because of the confusion thus caused. In the midst of it I
sometimes feel a rush of an unlikely, unbecoming violence."

To Eleanor, October 23, 1858, from Lexington

*I am here for a few days only. I find the very aura of the whole
country changed and I have a feeling that we are divided by an issue that will not stand division. It is a dangerous thing to meddle
with so young an article as our democracy (even though I do not
think that many of our people even know what the word means).
But as A[lexis] de T[ocqueville] said, "no new idea will ever remain in its original form," merely paraphrasing Montaigne's
"Nothing endangers a state except innovation; change alone leads
to injustice and tyranny." Hardly either are original in their senti-
ments as Machiavelli said it long before, coming much nearer the
seed of the matter, with "let no one who begins an innovation in a
state expect that he shall stop it at his pleasure or regulate it according to his [original?] intention." I suppose I am too concerned.
Yet we stand to lose so much of a peace that few people have ever
known.*

A hint of presentement or prophecy is apparent in a melan-
choly comment in the next letter:

To Carrie, October 29, 1858, from "The Lake"

*In this climate the doors to the ballroom already stick when the
weather is damp (no fault of Mr. Sloan). I am enjoying the near
perfection of my house, though. Often when my menage is asleep I
go from my bedroom into the enormous space [of the ballroom]
and think how colorful, how beautiful it will be when put to its
proper use—but sometimes on these nights I walk to its windows
and the balcony overlooking the park and Lake and am saddened*

*beyond expression at the quietness; there is an expectancy, as if
waiting for desolation to set in.*

In the extant letters, up to this date, hardly any note of fatal-
ism has appeared. Rage, yes. Regret, yes. But never bleakness
or drabness. Yet something elusive, provocative, and prophetic
begins to appear in all of her correspondence now. In another
letter she continues in the same mood:

*What is going to become of it all—what, exactly, here? Why
here at the end of the earth (to many)? It is the ending of an era
and much of the blame goes to that Stowe woman. I see little of
Charlie these days; it is perhaps as well.*

We gather from contemporary accounts that Margaret's husband, "Charlie" Dudley, was an amiable, handsome, lazy, aimless man. He seldom did more than read or ride over the plantation between juleps. Margaret could hear the Johnson family's
"We told you so," but this she ignored.

[To Carrie], November 10 [1858], from Lake Washington

*This has been a year of no small catastrophes for those of us who
depend on our land. The ugly Monster, the river, has given us
nothing but trouble. Along with it all, Claude has blown up a strip
of his plantation north of here and made himself an island—and
at the same time created his own lake [Lee?]. I only wish he had
used some of the powder to blow that ratty remnant of humanity,
Stephen Douglas, off his place near Silver Lake (I wonder if he
really owned it or if it was come by through the good graces of my
ill-advised brother Matt?)*

To Samuel Sloan, November 1858, from Lake Washington

*I have just seen the beautiful Wayside house. It has given me a
few ideas that we might incorporate in the other outbuildings. As*

far as the children are concerned, I think we should plan another *wing!*

To Samuel Sloan, November 25, 1858, from Lake Washington

I am still receiving remarks concerning the absence of stairs in the central hall. This does not change my opinion at all. But I do admit that it would benefit from the installation of the statuary planned for it, and about which I implore you to make immediate inquiries. (After all I have now paid a good sum for the two pieces.) No, the stairway does not bother me at all. You agreed with me on keeping the entrance simple and as for as I am concerned stairs are merely a hazard for young and old alike. I am quite content with the lack of symmetry, with the main stair hall where it is—and the back stairs in the other wing. Hoofing it up and down is never the essence of dignity at best.

To Samuel Sloan, December 7, 1858, from Lake Washington

I seem to be bombarding you with letters of late. But I feel I must write while I remember to tell you how very fortunate we were to have the suggestion of using Mr. Scudamore for the plaster work in my house. Each time I see the medallions for the chandeliers and the cornices in all the rooms I am astounded at the beauty of his art. It could have been so obtrusive and heavy and yet it appears as light as filigree at times. I hope that Dr. Nutt will use him in the house he is planning in Natchez; after all, Mr. Scudamore is from the same area, and it would be so simple and I am sure that H[aller] N[utt] would look far and wide before finding anyone of his ability and taste.

To Samuel Sloan, December 14, 1858, from Lake Washington

I am once more among my own and feel not particularly better for it. If it were not for watching YOUR *house grow I think I should have gone mad with* ennui *of the past two years . . . and the trip north was most disillusioning. . . . I have been having a feast of Sir Francis Bacon (Lady L. sent me a new, beautiful copy —far more legible than the one in father's library). Sir F. strikes at our times so accurately that I sometimes think he might be in the next room. There is so much truth in his "never forget that there are the sins of the times as well as the sins of men." and even more pertinent with what I suffered through* TWICE *with that Mrs. Stowe. And he repeats the Machiavellian warning: "Innovations are dangerous beyond foresight." Do you suppose* THAT *woman ever read anything beyond those family sermons and the Bible? She is unbelievably narrow and dull.*

To Samuel Sloan, April 3, 1859, from Lake Washington

. . . the house, even with some items still missing, is proving a joy. But where is my Diana and H.? [Hermes? Hercules?]

To Carrie, April 1859, from Mount Holly (at LAST)

I rode down to the McCalebs' (stopping for a short visit with M. at Linden—what a drab house!) to see the new *church organ. I was prevailed upon to try it (you could not have kept me away with a derringer) and find it* satisfactory, *but certainly not of a resonance that I would have it possess. Perhaps time will mellow it —as it is supposed to do most of us. The organ looks well, but often an hysterical woman does also; certain stops or combinations make me cringe. I hope that M. or Miss S. can produce more from it than I.*

To Carrie, May [1859?]

I have been most entertained by having Victor G. A. [Audubon] here for the past week. A most dedicated and interesting man . . . I find his work—and of course, his father's—most fascinating. Their [V. G. and J. W. Audubon] being able to finish their father's uncompleted work is a wonderful thing . . . I have many plates here in my new library. He is out with Tom each day, in the forests back of the plantation (forests which I suppose I own), looking for the unusual.

To Carrie, May 1859, from Mount Holly

The only respectable season that the south has to offer is upon us—or is this true everywhere? Last fall's rather lavish indulgence in plants is paying off now with early roses—Damasks, Mosses, Chinas, Teas, and the rest. Some hungry creatures consumed half I set out in October; I only hope they met their Maker surrounded by blossoms. My walled garden is still not done although I have several times marked it off and started Robbie and Jim digging. Yet something always interferes—unpredictable weather, a child's illness, a houseparty that goes on for longer than it should. The deer have made spindles of many of my plantings of larger shrubs and trees. But the animals are so beautiful and tame I can not quarrel with them! Only plant more and try to give them some protection.

Matt came down from Chatham and we had a strained talk over an extraordinarily chilly julep; although a hot May day there was frost everywhere. I sometimes think that we did not even have the same parents, so divergent are our ages and views on EVERY-THING. I can always hope there was some cheery skulking about in the dark . . . there was always dear Uncle Richard as an example of what can be done if you set your mind to it.

How I long to go north again! But there is so much to do here now, from day to day. Thos. [Redd?] takes most of the problems from me when they apply to the land, but the household is difficult to contend with—with Charlie's complacence and stimulating habits; he is little or no help and requires more watching than any of the children.

To Carrie, May 10 [1859], from Mount Holly

Mr. Sloan stopped here on his way to Natchez and Dr. Nutt's

*proposed house. It was delightful to see him. A most remarkable
and gentle man. We are all quite well except for being somewhat
shocked and prostrated over Aunt Ray's death. But the fever
which we had so hoped was diminishing now seems to strike without warning, anyone, anywhere. She was about the last of my
favorite relatives who actually had a brain and knew what to do
with it, except rattle and rant.*

*The news from your corner of the nation only strengthens my
original contention. We are heading into a very dark period, indeed. President B[uchanan] seems unable to cope; I could have
told you that the second time I met him. But he has his problems
with so much dissent in the Congress. There were the days when
half our present politicians would have been boiled in oil. Justice
as conceived by Coke [Queen Elizabeth I's minister] with all the
circus of trial by jury is just so much dawdling.*

To Carrie, June 5, 1859, from Lake Washington

*I seldom weep but I have shut myself away from my family for
two days. I shall be thankful for my foresight and direct action regarding my slaves last year—not that it has changed anything but
the attitude of the community towards my person: but hell take
them, family, friends, or foe—and that dreary, deranged, reli-
gious fanatic HBS. My great depression is over the death of Nettie, the slave girl I brought from Kentucky and who throughout my
whole life has been my closest friend: she was indignant with me
only once—when I told her she was free. I shall never forget her
look when she said, "So's you no longer wants me?" I did so
"wants" her and hope I was able to prove it in this past, brief year.
She was perfectly well and her old laughing self last week. Over-
night she became ill. I sent to Canton for the best doctor (Charlie
conceded on this) but there was nothing he could do. I sat with her
for three days and nights and was with her at the end.*

I am not one to wring my hands and fall on my face or back-

wards with the vapors in my unadulterated grief. But Nettie's death has left me bereft—utterly bereft.

Charlie now looks at me as if my mind were affected; little can HE *ever know or feel or be. Oh, what a self-indulgent, compassionless world! What a fool I have been! Dr. Ben [Dudley]—as would Dr. Warfield, understands, but here I am cut off from people of great sensibilities—the father so often has not the gumption of the child. I fear Charlie has least of all.*

To Eleanor, June 8, 1859, from "The Lake"

This is our season of great satisfaction. But I have sustained such a personal loss in my beloved Nettie that I can not see much of the beauty around me. But I thank God I started planting the park seven years ago so that the house (now built) does not resemble a trunk standing in a field. Some of the trees are already huge and I have Job and another man working on what is to be my rose garden, Deo volente. One of my favorite lake-side cypress was struck by lightning a few weeks ago and seems to be dying. There are many others but this one I marked as being particularly beautiful.

I wish that I might once more see you and your husband. The times seem so unsettled and one never knows what the next few months will bring. I, who am not afraid of Astoreth or her cohorts, am very skittish about even going as far away as Lexington or Louisville. My responsibilities here are great and I should be worried the whole time although I know my married sisters L. or E. would be most capable in holding things together.

The girls are quite independent young ladies now—they have grown so fast; it is the boys for whom I am in the most trepidation.

Do let me know what your husband thinks of our chances for a peaceful solution. You know my views and so does he. I trust few people more and am glad that his eastern holdings were not affected by the California catastrophe [failure of the California bank with which William Sherman was associated]. How well I remem-

ber our good times together in the New Orleans "mausoleum!"
Yet, do you know that there are times when I now miss the house
there?

To Carrie, June 16, 1859, from Mount Holly

I suppose that even to you, my mentioning Nettie's death a second time must make you doubt my mind, but it is a loss to which I can not become reconciled. One recants so much in the face of oblivion, so I am glad that I am not left with guilt, for I gave her as much as I gave any child or sister. I shall never find such devotion —and it would have been that way had I clothed her in fig leaves and made her sleep with Charlie's hounds. I have lost a friend.

To Carrie, July 1859, from Mount Holly

Lillie, my oldest child, returned from Chatham a much wiser fourteen year old. I do not think she will be intent on going again; I have not asked too many questions but I can only surmise that she and that blustering brother of mine disagreed intensely. I would like to know the reason. L. has now gone through the complete register of the family in these parts; a tiff with [?] Worthington was all she needed in that direction. Now the Johnsons and the Wards have been an anathema to her for some time. Strangely, we can communicate but seldom—even though we, somehow, must resemble each other to a great degree. Thank God, she idealizes Mrs. Turnbull and the Morgans.

They are quite concerned over the price of the new organ; it has not yet been settled. Mr. McCaleb gave the land; I do not see why he should do more. Rather than let the place run into trouble I shall contribute whatever they still need. I am quite fond of the Hampton boys, and while the elder Wade Hampton is intelligent and charming he has a chilled arrogance that is hardly justified in his background. It is just this side of the theatrical. Mrs. Burnett [Fanny Kemble] could do better.

Margaret finally did supply the remaining funds, although she was beginning to be disenchanted with the whole matter of the church. She thought the Bishop Otey "a tiresome speaker and a plaintive man." In regard to the foregoing (after a missing passage), she says, "I had words with Wade—I knew it long ago. He is stubborn and, at times, a very dense man, for all his flattery."

To Eleanor, 1859, from Princeton, Mississippi

Times goes swiftly here. I am much confused when it comes to some details of my business affairs with father. I would like to see Mr. Sherman—and thank God each day that he is, even at a distance, there to advise me.

So that brilliant man is dead! Alex de Tocqueville—France has not many to lose, and this great one so well understood us, our ambitions and our frailties. I feel that so far as France is concerned Louis N. is but a figurehead and that his government will go the way that it did under a certain other member of his family.

To Samuel Sloan, September 12, 1859, from Mount Holly

I have made a discovery, and a friend. One of your labor "force"—Paolo! The young man from Ravenna! He became brightly alive when I told him that I had been to Italy not too many years ago. I have had him in several times to play for me—God help me if Louis ever hears of it, but I think P. plays equally as well. Such a glowing, classic face—such talent in his plaster work and his music.

When I think of how these men are treated in my land I am riled beyond reason—and I feel it all jealousy and on the part of black and white, for these—ours—are lazy, morbid men of vagrant and slight abilities, not within a thousand miles of possessing genius. They grumble when they see someone who does or knows more then they do, and are aggravated beyond speech at a foreign accent (and THEY jar the English language so as to make it unintelligible). As much as I think of them myself, the colored race has

done more to mutilate English with their tribal variations—and
pass it on to the white man—than any people I know.

To Samuel Sloan, December 17, 1859, from Mount Holly

This has been a most joyous time of year for us—although the
year itself, just about past, left much to be desired. Yet your contri-
bution to the perfection of this house has helped us over all other
difficult matters. We have had several large celebrations here dur-
ing the holidays, some guests coming considerable distances, Dr.
and Mrs. Nutt, Mr. Percy and his handsome son [William Alex-
ander Percy the first?], the two Harris brothers from Vicksburg
and the younger Audubon boy. Miss Meade came back from Nat-
chez and asked [of] you and your family. Matt was, of course, not
seen, and father and much of the family were in Kentucky, but
Lou and Mary Bell appeared and the Worthingtons. Most of the
rest of the Lake community came in at some time or other. A rela-
tion of the Harris's—at least I think she is—whom I met in Vicks-
burg last, would not come because she had "heard of the amounts
of spirits consumed and the dancing!" I believe you met her through
the Rollins and Yergers.

As for Margaret's nearest neighbors (more cousins): "The
Wards are in Kentucky for reasons known only to themselves
and God. I suppose that Junius is having to extricate Robert or
one of his children from some new misadventure—a flighty lot."

To Carrie, March 11 [1860], from New Orleans

James Gallier's new Opera House should make New Orleans
proud. It is quite beautiful and, so far, the performances have been
most acceptable, although the premier in December [Rossini's
William Tell] was most commonplace.

On the same theme she adds later:

I have heard so much good music here, some for the first time in

this country: Donizetti's L'Elisir d'Amore—*so long ago!* —
Halevy's La Juive, *and most unforgettable, Meyerbeer's* La Pro-
phète. *Then Jenny Lind, whom we heard in London, in New
York, and finally in New Orleans [1859].*

To Samuel Sloan, April 1, 1860, from Mount Holly

*As one of my closest and dearest friends what do you think will
come of this question of emancipation as it might pertain to war?
What both sides would lose would be irretrievable. I am sure that
New England is to blame for working the bellows upon the spark.
It took that ignoramus, know-it-all Mrs. Stowe, to really fan the
fire. A few years in Cincinnati and a week in Kentucky and she
writes a tiresome, inflammatory book—with great authority—
and now a second one (Dred)! I try to keep an open mind, but
when I see mealy-mouthing, glory to Godding, being taken as
Gospel from a silly New Englander—it almost kills me.*

*I, personally, have been done with slavery from my beginning
—officially and possibly to my downfall, for two years. My father
pontificates on my act and suffers heavily for me with long foreboding, heavy-lidded glances—along with my granite-brained brother
—but no matter now, we are all in it together, north and south
alike.*

*I have witnessed more injustice to the Negro in the north than I
have ever seen in the south. But war—it might mean an end to us.
Not only of us but of everything. We shall be delighted to see you
when you come down on your way to Dr. Nutt's next month.*

To Carrie, April 3, 1860, from Mount Holly

*No one could know but by looking at me how much good your
visit did for me—for all of us. I had despaired of ever making contact with my friends in the north and east; for over a year I have
held grave doubts, and although your letters and a few from others
there and in New York have kept me informed about the world as I
once knew it, I somehow never expect to see any of it again. Yet it*

all comes back to me through you! How good of you to come! And you saw Charlie at his best, for he had "reformed" to a slight extent, even though now he is brooding over his interests in Kentucky and perhaps over other matters of which I know nothing. Men are enigmas—sometimes, I feel, even to themselves.

It was so good to have word of the dear Sloans and now you can tell them of my happiness with his creation. I hear many things have gone wrong with Dr. Nutt's plans for his extraordinary mansion in Natchez; I fear for its future if everything goes the way that it is reported to be doing. These great meetings, the states themselves, Washington . . . nothing good can come of them.

To Samuel Sloan, April 10, 1860, from Mount Holly

Your good letter was just delivered. I can but comment once more on the simplicity and elegance of the wide stairway in its own hallway. Now there is only the statuary lacking in the main hall; for the present I have covered the two niches with tapestries with a commode below. It is but a temporary solution.

Later:

I am not pleased with the chandeliers but that has nothing to do with you. I should have let you select new ones for me and not tried to fit the ones from the house in New Orleans into this one; they are too bizarre and look as if they belong in a hotel, a bank, or store. Weight and size do not make for perfection of design. And then, I am still without hope that the glazing for the conservatory will ever arrive. I feel that it must have gone down in one of our too frequent river disasters.

Our country seems to be struggling through such a miasma that I suppose I should not fret over so small a matter. Yet this bothers me—as much as the temporary mantels that we had to install; the latter seem fit for a small child's or small maid's room.

You were quite right about the ballroom receiving sufficient heat from the rest of the house. Both the windows opening onto the bal-

cony overlooking the lake and the ones in the musician's alcove [the "musicians' alcove" measures about 13 x 23 feet] had to be opened on each occasion of a ball, even though the weather was unusually chill. I had been afraid of the draughts—somewhat like those that occur in some English houses I could name. But you, as usual, were correct.

I was most distressed to hear that you were having difficulties in finding anyone with enough brains to lay a brick properly and do plaster work in our state. All this, for continuing the work on Dr. Nutt's house. I know the problem you had in getting people to make the journey when my house was in progress and had hoped that somehow, someone would have learned a trade—other than squawking hymns or moaning their own dismal music to Almighty God. I was lucky in the labor you found in the north for me; the work is meticulously done—what wonderful craftsmen and so little appreciated!

To Samuel Sloan [1860 or later], from Mount Holly

. . . my cousin Sallie Ward. Her portrait by Healy is very pretty. But it seems to simper. No comparison in us—but my picture by him has dignity (a thing I usually abhor). Her house in New Orleans has taken on an even grander air—imperial it seems to me. I can never applaud or be one with the multitude, the common man, but I do think she is losing sight of the earth itself at times.

To Carrie, June 6, 1860, from Mount Holly

I have retired to my rooms for what I hope is the rest of the day, but I shall not try to command your attention with idle female chatter.

Later:

I was interrupted by Thos. [Redd?] who brought good news about last year's successful planting and crop. The children have *been unusually trying and Charlie has distinguished himself by be-ing more inebriated at two in the afternoon than he usually is at two in the morning. He did not appear for dinner, so Eugene and his sister, Johnson, Lillie, William and I had a delightful dinner to ourselves.*

New Orleans and the north had somewhat spoiled Margaret's taste for "southern" cooking, so it may have been the children around her who made the meal "delightful" and not the food, for she goes on to say:

I miss New Orleans most, I sometimes think, because of the ex-cellent cuisine. The appreciation of simplicity is one of the lesser arts, I am sure—and plantation cooking is much too highly praised. I fear that I have too much of Epicurus in me, but then I always did have a place in my heart for anything Greek.

Do you remember (how could you forget, you dear woman!) that ludicrous ride on that ass, to Delphi? And my acute repulsion of feta and goat's milk? And how furious I was that after thou-sands of miles of travel I found that a woman could not ascend to Mount Athos? The last still riles me.

Sooner or later women will be on a level with men in all matters but we are far from that today. My cousin, Sallie Ward, seems to have made more progress in that sort of emancipation than any fe-male I know. But her efforts are through flightiness and folly and little thought for others or any worthwhile thing—utterly brain-less.

To Carrie, June 1860, from Mount Holly

I am so embroiled in a problem not my own. Not really em-broiled, but I should like to be. It is strangely satisfying to a woman to be able to say, "I told you so!" It's Sarah Miller—you remem-ber I told you she had married much against everyone's better judgment. (I would say just because of everyone's judgment.) The man came from my least favorite nationality or race—a pig-

headed, obtuse, bigoted, arrogant German. And to make it worse,
a nobody. I do not hold with every opinion about class distinction,
but I know a dreary [undecipherable] when I see one. And Sarah
got him.

Now two years and one child later it becomes apparent that she
has forgotten one of the commandments. The one regarding "no
other God before me." She has made that fool an idol. Do not
criticize him, do not dare disagree with his mundane, banal, bigoted opinions. She will never speak to anyone who does so. Because of this he has alienated all her old friends—some family
friends for generations. I have never been so irritated at having to
sit and watch complete nervous devastation—and social ruin. I
told her frankly that I would always be glad to have her here but I
would be happier if her husband stayed at home. As a result I am
now an outcast.

There is nothing so sure to make a marriage occur or last as to
oppose it; S. knows as well as anyone that NP is utterly objection-
able. But woe, woe, woe to anyone who does not agree with his
common opinions.

To Carrie, December 1860, from Mount Holly

Perhaps God is looking after us or at least dealing with the country's problems in a left-handed way. The oily little beast did not get
to be President, even though he did have the Democrats on the run
for a while. If he had been elected I would definitely have sold my
property and my beautiful house and gone to England. Preserving
the peace, indeed. Kansas was quite an example. Oh, I loathed
that man on first sight!

Stephen A. Douglas probably never had a more violent oppo-
nent than Margaret.

To Carrie, [near Christmas] 1860, from Mount Holly

For a lark I let the children open many of the cases from the
New Orleans house, so long stored. They have come across some

delectable items and at this time I feel so happy for them. Christmas has been a most distraught season for me this year—so frustrating. For although I could even buy Oliver Morgan and his complete holdings (and most of father's, for that matter) and although James' old investments have paid off handsomely, there is little to be had. *This part of our country remains something of a material (and intellectual) desert.*

But all considered, it has been a diverting time and I have gently suggested passing many things along to our help, and they—the children—have received much pleasure in GIVING. *That pleases me. The only grumbling I hear is from Charlie; were you not a Lady and I not a Lady, I would air my view on that* LOUDLY. *He only seemed pleased when the gun arrived from England, by way of Sir Charles.*

Women have such small say—and from what I witness in both local and national politics I think it the root of the certain downfall of our country. Except for certain doubtful physical attributes, men are not really appealing when one witnesses the insane muddle they have led us into—relegating us to the parlor, the vapors, childbearing, and even (for our own good, they say) from the problems of our own properties. I recently had to tell Thos. exactly what I thought of that. Since then he has been most pliable and diligent in bringing to me even the slightest disorder.

Young Anthony R. came over to talk with me and Eugene in the late evening of yesterday—what a beautiful mind! He and Eugene are much taken with each other—and with Josephine!

To Carrie, January 20, 1861, from Mount Holly

So Alabama has played the fool and stuck with the three other insane states, and disengaged herself from the Union. She will, even as Mississippi and the others, pay dearly for such a gesture. There are meetings and riots everywhere, north and south, as well there should be. I hear that New Englanders (what hypocrites they are!) often side with the more misinformed, stubborn, bigoted and foolhardy southerners. Of course, they would do so—how did they get their money, aside from fish peddling and witch hunting? I can not abide the holier than God mind of Pilgrims and Puritans.

To Carrie, January 1861, from Mount Holly

I do not think that my state of mind can be healthy. In the midst of a thousand other [arguments?] I have almost discovered that the papers given to my slaves (by way of father) are probably not legal in this God-forsaken state. It is a terrible thing if this is so, for the few that have left may have run into insurmountable difficulties with no way to reach me. I have consulted the ones that are here and asked them to be patient until I find out. When I do and if my suspicions are correct I shall take this country and state to pieces; it would not take much for me to refuse to ever see father and mother again, and Matt knows better than to ever show his face again. Charlie may be in this, too—anything to dupe "old missy."
Conditions seem to grow worse by every post.

To Carrie [1861], from Mount Holly

You mentioned Mr. Stephen Foster as a part of our feeble music —I agree with you in this case. For although I liked him when I met his wife, Jane McDowell, I felt his music merely written to play upon sentimental and credulous fools. I do not consider it anything resembling prestige to come from the same state. Poor Jane—he is a burden that she must bear.

Later:

"My Old Kentucky Home" is a Travesty. And "Old Folks at Home" simply puling. I heard that the poor Fosters are in desperate straits in New York (his drinking, as usual, has put them there). I wonder through whom I might quietly do something for them?

To Samuel Sloan, May 5, 1861, from Mount Holly

I have heard of your difficulties with Dr. Nutt's house in Nat-

chez so I shall say no more regarding Mount Holly and be thank-ful that it was thus far completed before we plunged into what seems complete chaos. I feel so much for poor, disillusioned Dr. Nutt and Julia, for that house had been their dream.

I can only hope that Paolo [see p. 100] was safe in the North and stays there. What bigots our men are. Fight? Cats could do better on a fence.

The idea of harassing workmen, bent on their honest en-deavors, is more than I can understand. I feel, at times, that the human race is a filthy mistake.

Margaret had just heard of the threats against, and ill treatment of, the workmen—all artisans in their own various lines—that were brought from the north for work on Longwood. It was the general populace and their "ideals" that finally brought the project to an end. The vehemence was unbelievable; the resent-ment against people who merely spoke with an accent (mainly Greeks and Italians) went to incredible ends. Some barely es-caped with their lives. The whole matter sounds absurd, unrea-sonable, for the south at no point—outside of a scattered few in the endless forests and in a few cosmopolitan centers such as New Orleans and Louisville—possessed many artisans with the skills of these men, trained, first or second generations, in Eu-rope with its centuries of traditions. In reviewing letters (above) and records of the period, one finds that the resentment made them completely isolated. They were rejected by the literate and illiterate alike; even the black, still absorbed in his African background, ignorance, and cults (and possibly resenting the possession of valuable skills, among other things) considered them menacing interlopers.

Among other examples, the factors that surrounded the fate of Longwood was probably what led a man like George Temple-ton Strong of New York to assert, "The South to the North is nearly what the savage Gaelic race of the Highlands was to London *tempore* William and Mary . . . a few fine specimens have given them a prestige the class don't deserve. . . . The North are a busy money-making democracy. . . . A notion here has got footing that 'Southern gentlemen' are a high bred chivalric aristocracy, something like Louis XIV's noblesse, with grave faults, to be most sure, but on the whole very gallant and generous, regulating themselves by 'codes of honor' (that are *wrong*, of course, but very grand); not rich, but surrounded by all the elements of real refinement. Whereas I believe they are, in fact, a race lazy, ignorant, coarse, sensual, swaggering, sordid, beggarly barbarians, bullying white men and breeding little niggers for sale."

Margaret Erwin had met Mr. Strong. If these views of his were put forth at the time, I am sure that so long as he did not class New England as the North, they were in complete accord. To her, New England was still "a land of witch hunters and fishwives."

Strong, as a northerner, was not alone in his bleak evaluation of the south and its inhabitants. He had traveled (almost as much as Harriet Martineau, Mrs. Trollope, and Mrs. Kemble) throughout the south. His knowledge of the building of Longwood may be an example from which he may (or may not) have gathered some fuel; in any case, the mores and attitudes of the southerner are documented somewhat in the letters between Sloan and Haller Nutt, which concern the (eventually) insurmountable difficulties encountered in constructing Longwood. (This correspondence is in the Archives of the Henry E. Huntington Library and Museum in San Marino, California.)

Throughout the last years of the Sloan-Nutt correspondence there are increasing allusions to the attitudes to any newcomer. Yet the finding of artisans or workmen of any aptitude in the south proved to snowball with multiple difficulties. In one letter to Sloan (March 18, 1860), Dr. Nutt wrote, "In regard to the brick masons I have I am sorry to say I can not rely on them much. One can fill in and the other can lay a tolerable wall if watched—but is so careless and takes so little pride in his work that he cannot be depended upon. So I think you ought to send out two reliable workmen and men that work fast. Fast workmen will stir up mine and then they do much better." Aside from this commentary on the quality of workmanship available, Dr. Nutt also drops an occasional hint regarding the relationships of the northern workmen and the southerners. In March, 1861, he wrote: "The bricklayers left on the 16th as I wrote you. On departure they left without my knowledge a card for our Natchez newspaper, which came out on the 19th and I was much surprised in going into town at everyone knowing it before I did. I did not like this at first but on reflection I was much pleased they did this. I send you a copy. It will show to Northern people that Phila. Mechanics have been South, and well treated, and not hanged." The card said: "Having terminated the brickwork for Dr. Haller Nutt's mansion we would take this method of tendering to that gentleman our sincere thanks for the very liberal and uniformly kind treatment extended to us during our sojourn with him; and to the citizens of Natchez generally, who have manifested to us the greatest courtesy during the intense excitement through which we have just passed."

This refutes, in part, allegations of obtuseness and narrow-mindedness in the South at this point; but it was generally thought to be the exception rather than the rule. The earlier objections to imported labor was mostly an ethnic matter. "The intense excitement through which we have just passed" is not further explained; it could not have been Fort Sumter, for that event did not occur until nearly four weeks after the men had left for the north.

The distant thunder of the approaching war had not prevented the near completion of Mount Holly, but by May of 1861, the reassurances of Dr. Nutt to Samuel Sloan must have had a dubious and hollow sound: "I wrote you yesterday that there was no danger in sending out men from the North and asking you to send the tinner (for the roof). In thinking it over I have thought to write you again—and say that affairs may grow more aggravating and possibly workmen from the North may be molested." It was left up to them to decide, and on June 20 Samuel Sloan wrote, "They declined going in consequence of the State of the country. All my talking and assurances proved of no avail. I then made effort to secure others, but all to no purpose. Fear seems to be the principal cause, no other."

Then, on December 2, 1861, Sloan wrote to Nutt: "It has been rumored that men have been withdrawn from working on your house . . . one of the workmen wrote from Cincinnati yesterday that such was the case and that they barely escaped [their lives or through lines] without giving any cause whatever."

To Samuel Sloan, May 1861, from Mount Holly

I regret that I can not accept your verdict of its being "fate" regarding Dr. Nutt's house, and I suffer deeply for all of us. I do not wish to pose as a Fanny Kemble version of Cassandra but I fear I saw the outcome of the indolent, stubborn, and more-often-than-not ignorant southern mind. Yet this is a human state that is not wholly belonging to the south. We have our foibles and our wrongs —but none so great as to deserve bringing about what our politicians have brought home to us.

You and I have agreed often that the fault lies with both sides and that Greed and Intolerance are the only things the North and South really have in common. For, if we depended for a time on slavery (and this I will never defend), then we must both admit that our mutual and amusing (northern) friend, old Mrs. F's fortune and beautiful house (and those of her daughters) in Cambridge, are built from the very planks of slave ships. I condone nothing on the part of friend or foe. I may die with a conscience outraged with my own sins (in reviewing them—aside from Cath-

*olic mumblings—what ARE my sins?) but not one will be of intol-
erance or ignorance.*

To Carrie, summer 1861, from Mount Holly

*So they have carted the old badger back to Les Invalides? I hope
he is satisfied. We only hear talk of soldiers and their movements
everywhere. Thank God I have not caught sight of one of either
side. On my property—as I wrote Eleanor and told her to tell William S—they will be promptly shot. By me.*

The "old badger" was Napoleon I, another one of Margaret's
pet hates. With her usual vehemence when speaking of him,
she refers to his body being brought back to Paris after being
buried for nineteen years on the island of St. Helena.

To Samuel Sloan, June 29, 1861, from Mount Holly

*There is little peace for us here, or anywhere. We no longer
have a government, I contend, and will continue to have none.
Surrounded by jackals and traitors, the President—the real President—has no power. I have just had my last drink with Matt and
told him to go home and stay there; I hope the goat drowns in a
julep.*

*I did so want to live to see the place "grown up," but my rose
garden is not yet, nor apt to be. The hall niches remain empty, the
balcony railings, still wood, need painting again. All this must
sound very shallow and muddle-brained to you. You did your
best. Somehow, somewhere, I must have failed. But poor Dr.
Nutt and the V's; compared, I was more than fortunate.*

To Carrie, October 1861, from Mount Holly

*Yesterday was quiet, and in a warm early autumn midday I felt
a need to escape. Charlie is very fettering. Joel and I rode over the
whole plantation for nearly three hours; I believe it was only the
second time that I have seen ALL of it. When I am out of doors,*

Joel or Job will not let me out of their sight. They both think the army is around the next bend in the road. It is so strange—they are both coal black, and distrust northerners beyond [description?].

In my thoughts while out, I considered the mounds, the Indian mounds, where they were said to bury their dead; others say they were built to save their families in time of flood. I do not know. We rode down to them. There is a grove on the largest, where I tied my horse, with Joel looking at me most disapprovingly (the Negroes think the mounds "hanted"). He rolled his eyes and got ready to defend me if I were attacked by something evil—seen or unseen.

Yet all I felt—for the moment, at least—was peace, and I indulged this rare feeling and time to the hilt to review what has happened, what is happening, what is going to happen. Yet I came back to the moment—the time and place—with no resolve. I am as lost as any. We've no Clays, no Jeffersons, no Websters to turn to—and when we had we paid but little attention to what they saw thundering towards us. But it was good to walk there and be alone for a time. I shall go again—if Joel will let me!

Johnson and William have been ill again. Lillie is visiting her husband's cousin in New Orleans. I had a letter from William S[herman]—really but a scrap—but all is well with my affairs in spite of his being caught in this military maze.

To Eleanor, December 1861, from Mount Holly

I was most touched by Junius Ward's gift of thirty of the ballroom chairs from his great house in Kentucky. They are most charming, quite delicate, in rosewood and gilt. I must tell Mr. Sloan how much they add to that mammoth (alas, seldom used) space. The Wards also gave me two pedestal tables which I appreciate, but the house now grows so full of furniture it will soon look enciente.

I am a little concerned over the Wards' generosity. Do you suppose they are contemplating having to leave their home there [in Kentucky] so soon after completing it? It makes one pause.

Ward Hall, as it is now known, was lost by the Wards, as Margaret feared.

To Samuel Sloan, January 3, 1862, from Mount Holly

> To think we are now separated by the ultimate folly fills me with an unspeakable loathing for both sides in this useless and destructive conflict. It is something that neither our children nor our children's children will ever live down. And all over a question that will never be resolved or acceptable in any way to the majority of our nation—or any nation except those of the jungle.
>
> If only we had been a hardier people—done without them, made less and cared less for what is Biblically known as "Plenty," been content with peace! We could have taken the people's resolution and, if affirmative, sent them right back where they came from—the dissenters, in any case. There are always the few exceptions, like my dear Nettie, who would be called traitors. But there have been traitors since Eden—and without them we probably would not have survived.

To Carrie, February 7, 1862, from Mount Holly

> There is so much unhappiness, so much tragedy all about. I shall never become resigned to the death of the young. It is hard for the old to look oblivion in the face—but those who have just begun to live! I am speechless! Our neighbors, the R's, just received word of the death of their oldest, Anthony, just twenty-three and an Apollo, unusual in that he combined all that was beautiful and sensitive with an innate wildness and a superior intelligence. He often came to talk with me—just with me! An old lady! [She was 42].
>
> I shall miss him and each day I expect to hear more of God's ill-considered behavior. Each day I come nearer to a new belief that may turn out to be a faith in NOTHING. Eye upon the sparrow, indeed! Perhaps in another world—but not this.

To Carrie, March 9, 1862, from Mount Holly

I suppose I should keep my grief for my own house, for we are really in for it, I fear. But I find that I am still desolated by the death of A[nthony] R. And others, too. I walked alone in the moonlight last night, all the way to the edge of the Lake. Never has it seemed so calm—and by this, and its beauty, I came to the sad conclusion that all our world is becoming a man-made charnel house. When I returned to the house some hours later, all was quiet and the light on the facade was dim and beautiful. As I let myself in, Joel roused himself, showing the whites of his eyes, then realizing it was only "missy," the white of his teeth. I have had a pallet made for him every night, just inside the door. Then I walked to the dining room for a glass of port and slowly made my way upstairs. Passing through the ballroom I thought of how little of the gaiety it has known for which it was built. I did not sleep until dawn.

To Carrie, March 25, 1862, from Mount Holly

There is a strange sense of expectancy round about . . . everyone here seems to be caught in it. Either that or a kind of somnambulistic lethargy. Perhaps one is kinder to the mind and the body than the other.

I have heard utterly nonsensical rumors regarding my father's attitude towards me; I cannot say that, knowing him, I am at all surprised if they are true. In any case they could not make less difference.

To Samuel Sloan, April 1862, from Mount Holly

I heard from Miss Meade (she is staying with me for some months) of Natchez, of how the end came so finally to Dr. Nutt's house. It must have been a terrible loss and disappointment to him and to you. I feel that you may have had other business in the locality that has gone the same way. I thank whatever gods there are left still stalking about that I was allowed to go this far with Mount Holly, and to enjoy it for the few brief years that I have.

All work was stopped on Longwood in 1862. Dr. Nutt died, and his family was housed in the nine rooms that were completed on the ground floor.

[To ?], May 1862, from Mount Holly

The whole irresponsible murder is coming closer to home. Last month, Corinth, in the northern part of the state, and all through Tennessee and up and down the river. How I wish I had taken every last child of ours to England and built my house there! Not that the English were guiltless of the slave trade—but through maturity of many minds it came to a logical end at a propitious time; it was the New Englanders who capitalized. I do not doubt that a hundred years from now a few hundred "proper" New Englanders will wallow in wealth as a result of what they now so heartily disapprove. I hear that one can pay another to go into the war for them . . . this, via New York. What brave men they have!

A page is missing, then:

Sallie Ward's only sensible act took place during the early days of her marriage to Timothy Bigelow Lawrence and showed that a woman in pants is sometimes more effectual than a man with or without. Her behavior was scandalous, yet, I can not help but laugh when I think of those pinch-mouthed old witch-hunters' expressions when she appeared in satin bloomers, a turban and pounds of jewels. You know how much I love New York and Philadelphia, but Washington I consider a slum and Boston lower than any ring in Dante's Hell. Yet I do like old Abbott [Lawrence] and Kitty.

Our news is not good. For a month there has been a formation of ships off the New Orleans coast. We are making what I consider feeble attempts to defend ourselves. How misled, how unprepared can men be?

To Carrie, June 1862, from Mount Holly

One never knows whether or not one's letters are getting through or whether one is just writing to while away these distracting times, and nothing more. We have little to report here and I suppose my letters would be confiscated and cut to bits if I were to write that little I do know—which, incidentally, is NOTHING. *We are isolated. I suppose many would wish to say the same. Black or white—or like Uncle Richard's cafe au lait Adeline and Imogene—the southern mind remains the same: unyielding, stubborn, and stagnant.*

Oh, we have our intelligent men. But of even these, so many are corrupt. I am sure you have your share in the North.

We know now that New Orleans was bombarded in April and little damage was caused. I am so glad we rid ourselves of that house—but what of our other property? I know much of history, and that most of history is made of, or is dependent upon, war. But I shall never accept it, nor will I ever accept the men who know precisely what they are doing.

Later:

Now we hear that Forts Jackson and St. Phillip have surrendered. To the waste of so many lives—and to what cause?

I know, de mortuis nil nisi bonum *and all that but I shudder to think what the evil little S.A.D. [Stephen A. Douglas, who died of fever in 1861] helped bring about, and I might as well include my brother Matt, recalcitrant and ugly in thought. I am beginning to think of my brother as one of the* smallest *men I have ever known. I am glad to be as far removed from Chatham as I am— and I wish we had an ocean between us. [?] is so sweet to be penned up with that pig.*

To Carrie, July 1, 1862, from Mount Holly

I am so cut off from music now that only through your news of it can I imagine what is happening. So glad that Mr. [George] Bristow's Symphony [in F# minor] went so well, and yours was

Part III—1851–1863

the first news I had of the death of Anthony Heinrich in Kentucky. Uncle Richard was such an admirer of his work with, and adaptions from, the Indians and their music; his, I hope, was a lasting service and will be appreciated by posterity.

Heinrich was a European musician who lived for many years in Louisville and undertook the notation of native Indian music. After a brief return to Europe he went back to Kentucky in 1837 and died there in 1861; Richard Johnson was his patron and friend.

[To ?], July 7, 1862, from Mount Holly

Little or no word comes to me from Kentucky or Nashville these awful days. We feel completely sealed off from the world. Charlie is better, but not well.

To Carrie, July 1862, from Mount Holly

I can not imagine where the terrible dreams I have originate, I who have never had much time for dreaming. In my sleep last night I saw this place leveled, and ran from tree to tree trying to find at least one child. But there was no one—child or adult. Each day I make a staunch resolution that I will not listen to one more word concerning this foolish war. Then I am overtaken by a woman's natural curiosity and fear.

To Carrie, July 1862, from Mount Holly

I'm not too well. I so soon tire of everything. That is not like me, and you know it. Perhaps with fall I shall be myself again. I so fear for Eugene, for he is in the foremost of it now. With every message I expect the worst.

I do hope the dear Sloans have not been caught in this malevolent web. It was true that Dr. Nutt's house was left but a shell, workmen and materials being impossible to obtain and retain.

Little Charlie fell down the nursery stairs yesterday and almost broke his leg. He is dragging around like Captain Lafitte on his

119

wooden one. Lillie is here now and is giving him so much attention that I fear he may continue it for the rest of his life. I shall see to that, giving them a few more days. Pampering is not a specialty at Mount Holly unless fully deserved. You must think me a heartless witch.

I see nothing to criticize in the exuberance that drinking brings —the release, the oblivion; but Wilkins [she called her husband by his middle name when she was particularly annoyed with him] carries it too far. Not one to be so vulgar as to compare husbands, but James was a gentleman. But Charles is often a drunken gentleman —and offensive. James was never that. I can only hope the tendencies are not inherited.

To Samuel Sloan, September 20, 1862, from Mount Holly

President Lincoln's statement to Mr. Greeley was most satisfactory to my mind, yet most contradictory. I would hate to think that he was merely elusive if not devious and a typical politician.

Her allusion to the president was in regard to Lincoln's answer to Greeley's question concerning the "perfect" solution to the slavery issue and the war. Lincoln had said, in part, "If I could save the Union without freeing any slaves I would do it, and if I could save it by freeing all the slaves I would do it; and if I could save it by freeing some and leaving others alone I would also do it."

Margaret added,

On rereading and considering it, I think it sounds either quite weak or utterly bewildered—for the latter I would not blame him. But we need neither quality in a man at the head of our government just now. I like to think he has been misquoted or misinterpreted, for I am his staunch supporter. Poor Mary—all this will do little for her.

[To ?], October 1862, from Mount Holly

120

It is all nearer. There has been some sort of confrontation at Iuka [Mississippi] and at Friar's Point. A letter came through from Alice [Lady L.] and they are in an uproar over our situation, so very concerned. How I should love to be in England with my brood. And my house—although for that, now I am sure I could find one equally to my liking.

To Carrie, October 1862, from Mount Holly

Alice wrote that they were all quite concerned over us—as well they should be—and that the rumors there were quite dreadful. I must quiet the poor dear as far as we, ourselves, are concerned. Her missive looked as though it had been opened and regummed several times in addition to stains that looked like those left by chewing tobacco, if not worse. How horrid! What we must endure to survive this fraudulent and childish war. Dear, dear Anthony —I can not get over it.

To Carrie, October 1862, from Mount Holly

To think we are related to that scoundrel Morgan [John Hunt Morgan]! I have now placed him in my private pantheon of hell along with father and Matt and a few others best left unmentioned.

John Hunt Morgan was the leader of Morgan's Raiders during the early days of the Civil War. Although Margaret groups him with her father and Matt, the whole of the Johnson family loathed Morgan and for once Margaret agreed with them.

[To Carrie], October 1, 1862, from Mount Holly

Along with all our other concerns is the rumor of a fresh out-break of cholera. We are fairly isolated, but I can not help but remember that father lost over thirty five of his slaves some years ago —that, too, began as country nattering but proved only too true.
I have just heard of the disaster of Antietam. We fall back everywhere.

121

[Torn page; to whom?], November 1862, from Mount Holly

> . . . *and if we lose we lose all, anyway. The Junius Wards live in terror for their possessions—that mass of plate, crystal, and china, and the beautiful Sheraton pieces they have. Some they could bury, as others are doing, but not the furniture, the Binghams, Healys, and Audubons.*
>
> *I, for one, will let all stay as it is—all except a few favorite and irreplaceable pieces such as Father Henry's [Henry Clay] few items of silver and the remnants of the blue and white china. And the antique head I bought in Rome (and at last have come to realize its value)—that I have buried, coming to the conclusion that a few more years in the earth can hardly create damage that some centuries did not. For the rest, the French and English furniture, it will stay in its place. The taborets and etagères will stay as arranged, and the portraits will be left on the wall until they are cut down or confiscated, if it comes to that. For all our pride here, in "our" work, it all seems so vain, so shallow now. We churn about so uselessly.*
>
> *Others, I know, have buried* ALL *their valuables. Perhaps it is wise. But I prefer to let come what will.*

To Carrie, November 8, 1862, from Mount Holly

> *To get away from the house and children today I rode to* Fair Oaks *to see my cousins, the Wards. Joel went with me; as I told you he will not let me out of his sight when I am out of doors. "Too danjus, missy, too danjus." I found Cousin George [Ward] in the depths as word had just come that Harrodsburg [Kentucky] had been badly damaged, and that things go badly for the family interests in Georgetown [Kentucky] and in Urbana [Ohio]. Also, in Kentucky, there has been considerable confrontation at Lexington and Versailles, and generally throughout Scott and Fayette Counties. It grows colder so suddenly this time of the year that I grew quite chilled and to keep warm walked my horse back to Mount*

Holly—*Joel and I leading our horses, both of us most silent.*

To Samuel Sloan, [late] 1862, from Mount Holly

I write under the most terrible emotional strain. I have been un-able to steady myself for two days. Somehow the message was de-layed, I don't know how, but three days ago it at last came through. My stepson, Eugene Erwin, was killed at Vicksburg in late August or early September. It is a sad day for us here at Mount Holly for nothing can ever be the same. Eugene was adored by all the chil-dren, and his wife, Josephine Russell. Johnson, his half-brother, seems to suffer most and comprehend least. I found J standing in front of E's bedroom, which is always kept ready for him and his family, completely immovable. Lillie is inconsolable. I shudder to think of the effect on Josephine.

How few years of happiness have we known in this house, the beautiful example of your work. It was to have meant so much to all of us, yet all has so far passed us by. Now I feel so much un-done, so useless. The war, this war in particular, has proven an evil, wasteful thing, and will grow even more so with time.

To Carrie, December 26, 1862, from Mount Holly

A most lamentable time for the adults this year. But the children and the darkies make so much of it, and we really are luckier than most, lacking nothing. I give wherever and whenever I see it needed and hope that Christmas was made brighter for the giving. Joel always finds a ham or two, several geese or a turkey; all else we have. Several friends from Vicksburg, Woodville and Natchez have managed to come to us. So we either cheer each other, or moan together. Somehow Eugene always seems near me, and I feel his going less. His death—so futile, so evil, so much in vain for a foolish cause.

There was a time when we saw much of the Morgans [in New Orleans] and now this has put an end to our seeing anyone. Wade [Hampton] has gone and Christopher (he married Mary Fitz-

*patrick, after all) and there is always the empty place that was
Anthony R's.*

How "friends from Vicksburg, Woodville and Natchez" ever
managed to get to Mount Holly for Christmas 1862 is a mystery.
The whole delta and hill country was writhing in first one battle
and then another. And how was Robert Ward, who died in
Helena, Arkansas, in September, 1862, carried back to Louisville for burial in the midst of the war? Only the Lake region—
and just that—seemed to have been forgotten and unmolested
by the conflict.

To Carrie, January 5, 1863, from Mount Holly

> *I hope I do not see the Wards for some time as I do not want to
> have to comment on Sallie Ward's latest caper. She is now, as you
> know, Mrs. S. W. Hunt. She deserted the home of Dr. Hunt and
> crossed over to the enemy for just one reason—she does not want
> to lose an inch off her petticoats, or be inconvenienced to the least
> extent.*
>
> *I understand she is going to write Mary [Lincoln]⁵ to get her to
> intercede for her regarding her piano and (probably hideous) chairs
> that have been caught up in the blockade. To think of whimpering
> about such things when we stand every chance of losing, or may
> have already lost, to the mercenary army. I cannot even speak of
> it further.*
>
> *I hear that Junius and Mattie have as little use for her as I, but
> they, at times, seem amused at her presumptiousness and imper-
> tinence in the face of God and man.*
>
> *It has been quite some time now since I have heard from Wil-
> liam Sherman except through New York and New Orleans.*

---

5. The letter from Sallie Ward to Mary Lincoln is not given verbatim; this is true of
Abraham Lincoln's reply to this same letter, as referred to him by his wife. They are
both to be found in *Lincoln and the Blue Grass Country* by William H. Townsend. The
lack of interest or the simple amenities of research have led to this and several other
items of considerable color being merely paraphrased and taken out of context.

I wish that I felt like taking the risk of going to Lexington to talk to Dr. Dudley about Wilkins. The situation is growing more untenable. The matter of heredity bothers me, and quite beyond that, Wilkins is an embarrassment to me and to all the children except little Charles, who thinks his father is "a funny man." There is nothing amusing about it, and I feel that Dr. Dudley might well have some advice; but it is a thing one does not write one's father-in-law about his son.

Margaret may not have heard directly from Sherman (he did have other activities on his mind) but she kept writing to—and hearing from —Eleanor.

To Eleanor, January 16, 1863, from Mount Holly

So we go into another year with nothing decisive about this war. No part of the conflict has occurred closer than ten miles to the north and eighteen or twenty to the south. What has happened in Kentucky I do not know. Word occasionally comes through, but how much one can believe it is hard to say.

She was interrupted, and continues later:

Our cousins and friends the Breckinridges, the Wards, Vileys and Flournoys have had to just about sacrifice their all. Cousin John [Breckinridge] is labeled a traitor[6] and many houses plundered, some destroyed. I doubt that there is much left in Kentucky for them to return to, but I do not know. One seems totally damned no matter which side of the fence one is on, and sitting on it makes a precarious perch. Thank God my feelings have long been known, far, wide, and loud.

My love to all in your household; I so dearly remember the days in New Orleans. There was not even a shadow—so far as we knew or cared—then.

6. This is strange, as Breckinridge has been variously ascribed as being one of the heroes of the New Market (Va.) battle. He did go into three years of exile in Europe but eventually returned to the United States.

125

Skirmishes took place all around (within a ten by twelve mile area)—Wayside, Greenville, along the river, Cary, Yazoo City, and other points, but never within miles of Mount Holly, Chatham, Linden, Otterburn, on or near Lake Washington, or the Shelby home on Lake Jackson.

To Carrie, January 18, 1863, from Mount Holly

> *I am still numbed by Eugene's death. And at the same time I have had a great fog cleared from my mind, and feel that, perhaps, death is the great solution, for our world—north or south—will never be the same, and I would not want to struggle through the morass of what will follow this war. I labored under the hope, even expectation, that the odious "Mr. Grant" would go under. But no longer, and I am sure that it is the south that will suffer most. But I have placed a most hideous curse on that dreary man and all that come after him.*

Later (January 19):

> *William T. S. was never far, or is perhaps so near even now. He has never failed as a friend and may be the reason for our complete isolation from the realities of our day. [It is more likely that the sparsely populated region was of little or no military value.] They have now come nearer, with trouble around the Worthingtons, not too far removed.*
>
> *I sometimes wonder if I do not overburden you with my problems. But it is such a relief to write, to reach out and know that there are those, even a world away, who do understand. I know that my house shall never be more complete than it is—my conservatory, my iron balconies, my walled rose garden. Yet it is the human loss I feel most—Eugene, Anthony, and all the others. Both these boys were like losing my very own; thank God they are too young.*

To Carrie, February 3, 1863, from Mount Holly

I understand the Union army has taken a woman named Belle Boyd, regarding her as a spy of considerable importance; I doubt that last most seriously. Yet I am glad to see women getting into this horrible political pudding. I hope that Miss—or Mrs. —Boyd gives them What For and gets away with murder. For that is all the gallant men are doing. Fighting for a Cause? The only causes are still Greed, Intolerance, and Insanity.

On January 1, 1863, Lincoln had finally issued the Emancipation Proclamation [in its finished form]; there was little in it that was unexpected, or not already known. It was a decisive measure concerning the war and only those states that had seceded from the Union; yet it did not signify that, the war once over, the South could not reinstate slavery after they rejoined the Union. Margaret's Mr. Lincoln was never devious, but even he could confuse issues and his public.

[To?], February 3, 1863, from Mount Holly

At last I know of Mr. Lincoln's January decision regarding slavery . . . it was a long time in the making, and I fear a trifle late.

To Carrie, February 8, 1863, from Mount Holly

I thank God every day that my William and Johnson are too young to get into this cauldron. Yet I can see they are puzzled by it, and Johnson feels Eugene's loss, even as I. Eugene's marriage to Josephine Russell was a distinct shock to him and for a long time he felt deserted, betrayed. But this senseless death may hurt the boy more than we now know. I suppose there are ways of losing more agonizing than death—but [none?] so final.
Wilkins returned last night from poker so far into his drink that I made him sleep in Eugene's old room; no one had gone there since his death. So just the sight of it on awakening may bring the

man to his senses, his sense of responsibility. He may think twice before repeating this performance.

I am quite amused in that I hear that father has made a new will, and left me completely out of it. No matter—I have more than he, so there may yet be logic in it; I only hope Lou, Em, and Mary Bell come in for the better part.

On January 10, 1862, Henry Johnson had taken care of his affairs in a lengthy document, a relic of the times that concerns this book only in one paragraph: "And it is further my will that my daughter, Margaret A. Dudley,[7] have no portion of my estate I having heretofore given her as much as I wish her to have."

Given was a strange word, since she had paid such a substantial sum ($100,000) for the plantation in December, 1854, a debt long since settled. It is doubtful that Margaret could have cared about this seeming disinheritance. But she did show concern for her sisters: Emily (by then a Mrs. Bartley), Louise (Mrs. Elly) and Mary Bell (the wife of General Blackburn, later Mrs. Carson). However, any worry about their well-being must have been eradicated in some way by the time Margaret made her own will (see Appendix, p.141), for only her husband and immediate children were mentioned.

To Carrie, March 1, 1863, from Mount Holly

Spring is supposedly a time of rebirth, but I feel little of it these days. All the news is bad and there is a terrible, bleak foreboding within me; in almost every family now death has left his mark. I walk through my park alone most of these days (conscious always that Joel has me somewhere in view. He is even armed these days —with a gun that Charlie gave him.) I go out alone for I wish to think. Sometimes a child joins me but I do not think that they find much comfort in "mother."

7. It is a mystery why her father used the initial "A."; she was christened Margaret Julia Johnson. There is no clue to this; she often used it herself; it is embossed on her family Bible and she used it in signing her will.

I smile when I think of how good my darkies are—yet I am concerned about them and hope to come to some solution before I die. Freedom for them is not enough—there is danger in it; they are children, primitive children, and a hundred years will not take care of that.

I am writing, sitting on a bench overlooking the Lake, so please overlook the scratching. I am well aware that Joel is not far away —who would have thought I would one day need a body guard! And who would want to harm one helpless old woman? [By this time she was 43.]

Later:

We know so little and imagine so much, and if our worst expectations are not realized it is more of an unfulfilled prophecy than relief that we feel.

To Samuel Sloan, March 17, 1863, from Mount Holly

Time wears on. I am very tired these days—you would not know me. The mirror says about the same thing—[yet?] I have not aged much, outwardly. Inwardly I feel but a husk, useless, deprived of my friends, happy of my children, but less than satisfied with my marital state. Even the little "good news" that seeps into us does not seem to cheer me—perhaps because there is no good news as long as this war goes on. I walked to the edge of the park overlooking the Lake (so peaceful this evening) and then looked back to our creation. The trees have grown and softened it and already it looks as though it has been there for many more years than it has, yet you must forgive me if I say that "our" creation has so little meaning now. Perhaps we built on sand, of a sort, and shall not weather this high, turbulent sea.

By early April her mood had changed and she wrote Carrie:

The artist recommended by Mr. Sloan (the one who did the

beautiful portrait of D[aniel] W[ebster][8] *quite outdid himself in the portrait of Lillie over a year ago. It turned out beautifully and we are awaiting* TWO *frames. There was some confusion—I ordered one and my son-in-law, Oliver Morgan, ordered one from New Orleans. Mine, from R. & M. in Louisville. They will probably arrive the same day, or they may never arrive at all due to the interference of this stupid and vicious war. Because of my lack of sympathy and general attitude, the behavior of some of my friends (and family!) toward me would make you cringe. I have no patience with the self-styled rebels—nor with the cowardly substitute-buying Unionists. Imagine buying a body!*

[To Carrie], April 10, 1863, from Mount Holly

The servants are terrified and I am trying to keep my own concern from the children. But there has been trouble at Wayside; our Worthington cousin's beautiful home was entered by northern soldiers and many valuable objects were taken. That brings the war closer.

That is about as close as the conflict ever came to Lake Washington. But this was disturbing enough for the interrelated families; and it was in this year that one of the Worthington brothers was killed by Federal soldiers on his own plantation. This senseless incident did more to harden the attitude of Washington County and that part of the state than any other single incident. Strange to relate, it was one of the Worthingtons who later saved the life of Colonel Dent, a relative of Julia Dent, wife of General Grant.

Surrounded by her children, the ones too young to be involved in the conflict, Margaret found herself going deeper into dark moods that were unfamiliar to her—and she realized it. She prophesied that the South (as she knew it) was lost forever. From this, one of her last discovered letters, it can be seen that

8. This portrait by John Pope is in the Charlestown, Massachusetts, townhall.

she never recovered from the death of her stepson, Andrew Eugene Erwin. From the time of his death an insidious melancholia crept into her everyday existence. Eugene had been the gayest of spirits to inhabit Mount Holly, except possibly for his father and Margaret herself. But the deaths of the people she loved best broke her reserves of humor and vivacity and she seemed to lose interest in life itself.

It is true that she suffered little immediate material loss. But it is apparent that material things mattered little to her compared to her loves, friendships, and hates. Yet now she couldn't even hate little "S. A. D."—he was two years dead of typhoid. She put up with Charles Dudley, possibly for the sake of their son, and because there was supposedly, in those times, no other easy and acceptable solution (although divorce, in normal days, was something that she might well have considered).

Her great adventures had not been just trips to England and the Continent; spread among them was the long-term planning and building of Mount Holly. There had been the greatest of pleasures in seeing it take form; now it had become merely the reminder of what might have been. As she walked through it, these thoughts are echoed in both the stated and the unsaid in her letters—through rooms that were now empty of all animation, a dining room that was filled with memories of a few years of holidays, a ballroom that revealed no more in its polished floor than the scarlet reflection of the late afternoon sun setting beyond the lake. The parlors saw few visitors, and the library became the sanctuary of the now ever-inebriated Charles Dudley. He had replaced most of Margaret's much prized books with his own choice of literary material. A contemporary once remarked when Charlie's books were mentioned, "Charlie Dudley's *library*? You mean one of the largest collection of dirty French novels in the state!"[9] It is, indeed, regretable that no

9. Capt. John Seymour McNeily. The "large library" seems to have been even more thoroughly dispersed. As mentioned before, Charlie Dudley's light and lively reading

one will ever know what his collection consisted of, if only to compare it with the pornographic output of our times. No mention is made of it in any papers concerning the settling of the estate. Many books from Mount Holly exist, but none of Charlie Dudley's.

Even young Charles seemed of little comfort to Margaret:

To Carrie, July 1863, from Mount Holly

> *I fear heredity so much. My mistake may yet be visited on my last child. I rejoice that Dr. Ben will never know the truth [about his son]. But appearances must still be kept up in this God-forsaken part of our land. The amenities of our once-happy life are being taken away from us; not all the money in the world can buy them back . . . gold has a hollow sound.*

[To ?], July 1863, from Mount Holly

> *We are losing, it seems, everywhere. I will have no part of it, but being a witness is distressing. A few days ago General Pemberton was defeated at Black River. Earlier in the month that execrable Grant cut down hundreds of our best men between Jackson and Vicksburg, and we now have small clashes as near as Greenville.*

Margaret was almost alone now, cut off from her family by choice. Only a few friends were allied with her neutral position and sympathies. The summer had moved on slowly, little work was accomplished, the blacks going slowly about their duties. President Lincoln advised Grant that Negro soldiers were an

---

matter disappeared; of Margaret's own library, there can be found the odd, occasional volume with the names of a Johnson, Erwin, or Ward inscribed. Even these have the occasional element of confusion: there are three separate volumes of Tom Moore's poems, a volume of Montaigne, of de Tocqueville, a history of England (from A.D 50 to George III), "Letters and Negotiations of the Count D'Estrades," a history of the Medici and a few novels of the day, including *Miss Thusa's Spinning Wheel*.

answer, perhaps, to shortening the hostilities; this did not prove true.

To Carrie, [late] July 1863, from Mount Holly

I do not know that this will reach you—we seem surrounded now that the omnipotent Mr. Grant has strangled Vicksburg. I heard by way of Bill [Harris? Mercer?] that many of the inhabitants have left their homes, taking to the hills, living in hovels and caves. I can not reconcile myself to the stubbornness and stupidity of their formidable relation, Mrs. L. She refused my invitation at the cost of safety to her and her family. I only did it, as you may well believe, as a gesture to the Harrises and a misplaced friendship, for she is a stupid, ranting, utterly mad woman. The Kennys and the Kleins (some of them) are in ENGLAND *(how I envy and admire them!).*

The battle at Port Gibson was a thing of which no army, no country, no faction can be proud.

I feel no better, but never one to complain I try not to let my own physical discomforts show in view of the terrible losses of others around me. My responsibilities with all the children are so great, and we are a family so scattered—that I do not know where to turn.

Perhaps God will at last take a hand and resolve some of our misfortunes. Facetious, dear, for His mind is not on this bellicose nation.

To Carrie, July 1863, from Lake Washington

I have just received word of the riots caused by the draft in the north. It has revived my spirits. No man should be made to fight in a war that he does not believe should be fought and no man should be made to fight at all. There is nothing so depressing as a romantic vision of war. I am completely attuned to the morality of an outright shooting of a despised figure—but when it is unknown brother against unknown brother I have no words.

But, my dear, these are our politicians; this is not a government. It is idiocy and fraud, and for all the dead there will be the many who make thousands from the conflict. They are the ones, if one could but prove it, who promote the general massacre. I must not write more—imagine me, weak; I feel more strange each day. I can ill afford an illness—I must live to see these terrible men who plunged us into this get their rewards.

But Margaret did not live to see the aftermath of the war. She had a strong premonition, one that was backed by some unspecified physical ailment. In late July, 1863, she was definitely unwell:

I feel a terrible oppression. The children make [me] nervous and I do not wish them to see me in this condition. I am sure that I have had a low fever for some time, so I must keep to myself for that reason if no other. I do so wish to see you and my friends there and pray that it may be so. I find myself hoping that I may once more see England—and yet I know it so vain, so foolish. Our real problems will come when the holocaust is over.

Like the following page of the above letter, the identity of the person to whom it was written is missing. It may well be among the last that she wrote, for on August 8, 1863—the very day that General Lee proposed to quit his command and was rejected by Jefferson Davis, Margaret lay barely conscious in her bedroom at Mount Holly—a cavernous front room opening into the ballroom and with a balcony overlooking the park and lake. Two days later she died. The cause was reported as yellow fever, but the insidious beginning and slow progress make it more probable that it was typhoid.

Most of her estranged family came to the brief ceremony that took place in the family cemetery near Chatham. Of her own immediate household, there were young William and Johnson Erwin (the latter now aged thirteen) and the two Charlie Dudleys, senior and junior. Some Turnbulls, Knoxes, McCalebs, Shelbys, Millers, and Wards made up the rest of the small gathering, along with many blacks from both Margaret's and neighboring plantations. The Hamptons and Smiths were away, as were the several Worthingtons. There is no record of whether the church itself was represented; but to her, we can be certain that it would not have mattered. (Now, even the small cemetery containing her grave, along with those of numerous other Johnsons, Wards, and Erwins, is gone—washed into the oblivion of Margaret's dear Lake Washington by the great flood of 1927.)

Following Margaret's death, her two Erwin sons, Johnson and William, and her second husband and son, the two Charles Dudleys, continued to live at Mount Holly. [10] Margaret's sister Louise (Mrs. Ely) was now a widow. (In 1868 she and Charles Wilkins Dudley, Margaret's widower, were married.) Johnson Erwin married his elder cousin Matilda Ward in 1874; William married Mary Stanford in 1878. William left Mount Holly with his wife, but Johnson and Matilda stayed on until 1880, sharing the house with the Dudleys. Then Johnson was "bought out," and he and Matilda moved to the last Junius Ward holding, Fair Oaks, (now Erwin) about a mile northwest of Mount Holly (and also on the lake). They moved before the deal was completed, in October, 1880.

Charles Dudley died in late December of that year, and Charles, Jr., was left alone in the big house, his stepmother having returned to Kentucky. Charles's habits, as his mother had feared, followed those of his father, and he died in 1893, unmarried, "as a result of overindulgence" following a dinner at a neighboring plantation, New Hope.

The history of Mount Holly is simple and rapid from that point on, well known locally and fully documented: it was

10. See the will in the Appendix.

bought by the Colwell family and they sold it to Colonel Huger Foote, Sr., in the mid-1880s. The Footes held it until 1903, when it was acquired by Dr. Albert Lee and his wife, Mary. On Mrs. Lee's death in 1956, the house was sold to the Gamble and Griffin families. Following Bonnie Griffin's marriage to John Cox, they continued to operate the plantation. But ultimately they found that the upkeep of Mount Holly was impractical, as they owned a town house in Greenville and had an additional business enterprise there. The Coxes generously offered Mount Holly to the State of Mississippi as a "model" plantation, but political finagling obstructed all chance of this. Of course Mount Holly would have become a most valuable example of a period and its people, with its furnishings restored and the buildings around it rebuilt and industries of a typical plantation of the period reconstituted.

Thereafter, Mr. and Mrs. Cox made a gift of the Mount Holly house to a local church. Though at first the church had little success with short-term tenants, the C. W. Woods family obtained a long lease for the property in 1979 and they are now engaged in restoring the house and grounds to their original state. What has been accomplished thus far in restoration has been done with taste and feeling for the original builder's intentions. Also, I am pleased to say that in 1973 Mount Holly was listed in the *National Register of Historic Places*, "thus making it the ninety-eighth Mississippi property so designated."

But chiefly Mount Holly stands as a monument to a unique spirit. During my early years when I lived on Lake Washington, before I went away to school, I never knew any of the occupants of Mount Holly well enough to even see the interior of the house. But I had become conscious of the personality that lay behind Mount Holly's creation and, through stories occasionally still current then that surrounded my great-grandmother, my interest was intense. From amusement at her behavior and the surface facts surrounding her life I became involved to an inescapable point. There was pride in passing the house, even in overhearing her name mentioned. She became a real person, one with whom I felt complete rapport, even though we were separated by nearly three-quarters of a century.

It was only after I left Mississippi that I started to experience moments of extreme satisfaction in recalling that I had known some of those persons who had actually known her. I always felt something of my grandfather's affection for her; he was thirteen when she died. I saw much of him when he was in his seventies. In his wife, Mattie, I sensed something entirely different, for although she obviously admired her mother-in-law in a way, there was a hesitancy, a faint radiation of antagonism, even jealousy. Perhaps she knew, even as a child in her teens, that Margaret "had her number."

With time and memory traveling back even further, I recalled an ancient and acerbic old gentleman who was Margaret's unfavorite brother, Matthew Johnson; he still lived in the decaying Johnson home, The Burn, at Chatham. Growing toward maturity, I became aware of artifacts at Erwin—portraits, silver, china, furniture—and I would recall that these once belonged to Margaret, so that even the inanimate took on a deeper, personal meaning for me.[11]

But Mount Holly itself continued to be the center of fascina-

11. Few items or artifacts—furniture, silver, china, glass, paintings, and other material—have survived through the Lake Washington Erwins. Much of the James Erwin silver is with the Washington, D.C., or Florida branches of the family. An enormous four-poster bed—Margaret Johnson's own (and in which she died), of mahogany with red silk hangings—is now owned by a Lake family having nothing whatsoever to do with its history. Four of Margaret's six children were born in it and all four of her Ward-Erwin grandchildren. Some of the ballroom chairs given her by Junius Ward, Sr., survive; so do a piece or two of blue and white china belonging to Henry Clay and a silver asparagus server. A portrait of "Lillie" (Or Julia Elizabeth) Erwin (Mrs. Oliver Morgan), painted by John Pope when the sitter was eighteen, is in the possession of the author. It was painted at Mount Holly, two years after the completion of the house. Sheraton, Duncan Phyfe, and many Regency and Louis XV pieces have long since been distributed among the Erwin descendants elsewhere. (It would be interesting to know where the antique head MJE bought in Rome now lies; it has never been found.)

tion. Each time I returned to the lake during school holidays or later vacations there grew an unrequited love for the place. This seemed to peak when I discovered the letters, more than a thousand miles away.

From there on I was hooked. Yet I came upon them too soon to appreciate their worth and importance. They amused me and yet I felt too deeply involved to ignore them. So my approach was jejune and careless, and my seeming lack of gratitude to the man who made them available to me now seems inexcusable. Several friends, seeing scraps of my efforts, hinted at their historical value, but for me the time was not opportune to recognize what they really represented. For soon afterward the world turned upside down and for four years I was occupied in the Royal Canadian Air Force, along with most of my generation in some branch of Allied service.

When I returned I recalled every so often the existence of the letters but living was disorganized and the world following the war was different from the one I had left. Yet Margaret Erwin was never out of my mind for long. There came a time when things grew more peaceful and I could devote experience and long-submerged thought and action to the woman who every year became more important to me. Even so, it took a hard shove on the part of a friend to get the project rolling.

Now each time I read these fragments of Margaret Erwin's correspondence I am struck by her unique personality, outspokeness, her lack of fear of God or man. I only wish that I could trace any of these qualities to any of her descendants. I share her views and am delighted when her prophecies, as dire as they usually were and are, come true, now in retrospect, now in tomorrow's newspaper. Has the abolition of slavery been replaced by anything that is either humane or practical? Have we had or do we have any men in politics to equal a Clay or a Webster? Her ethnic aversions were proven justified, as were her opinions on growing illiteracy and the darkening of national and international horizons.

Of her fears and hopes and outlook I think that what stands out most at this late date is her unswerving, immovable attitude to her fellow humans; forgiveness may have existed in her makeup but forgetfulness did not. In this I am reminded of an incident in Will Percy's *Lanterns on the Levee*, where after a desperate struggle between two Mississippi political parties the clash is finally over and dies down: "An old Klansman, one who, being educated, had no excuse for being one, asked me the other day why I'd never forgiven him. I had to answer: 'Forgiveness is easy. I really like you. The trouble is I've got your number and people's numbers don't change.'"[12] Margaret Erwin, with her strength of character, vision, and forebodings had the world's number. And the world's number doesn't change.

12. William Alexander Percy, *Lanterns on the Levee* (New York: Alfred A. Knopf, 1941), 241.

Appendix

Last will of Mrs. M. A. Dudley—Deced

In the year of our Lord 1863, I leave this day as my last will and testament, I give to my husband, Wilkins Dudley, 8.00 (dollars) and a fraction of land lying back of Mount Holly Plantation, also 15,000 dollars in notes and bonds, also, 5,000 dollars in Cash. The title of the land and the notes he has in his possession. Five years after my death I wish my property equally divided between my children, Lillie, Emma, Victor, Johnson, Willie, and Charley. I wish my Arkansas lands first sold, and then Mount Holly Plantation. The proceeds of the Mount Holly Plantation for five years after my death shall be appropriated to my first debts, the support of my family, and the remainder of the proceeds equally divided between my children. I leave my beloved husband executor of my estate. Witness my hand and seal

M. A. Dudley

No extant records of her Louisiana, Tennessee, or Kentucky lands have been found, nor are they mentioned in her will. It can only be presumed that they were disposed of before the war or else were lost as a result of it. The matter of the $8.00 above: was this a legal requirement of the time or what did it really mean; I have found no answer. Even with the monetary value of the day, $15,000 plus $5,000 and a "fraction" of Mount Holly Plantation seem a small amount to leave a "beloved husband." Perhaps Margaret had tongue-in-cheek and was only following the rigid, conventional lines of the day.

Appendix

Of some interest are bills, invoices, and receipts concerning either Mount Holly, its furnishings, or the activities of its occupants. Some will be particularly irritating or agonizing to those outraged by the economy of our times—by bills such as that from the Gayoso House, Memphis' leading hotel of the period; the date is October 1, 1858:

For Board 3 Days 7 Persons	$52.50
Washing $10.85 Do. $2.50	13.35
Meals to room	4.30
	$70.15

This bill was for the Oliver Morgan family (Lillie Erwin), on one of its many treks between Louisville and New Orleans, with their regular stopovers at Leota (or Washington) Landing to see Margaret Erwin.

A receipt from the Louisville and New Orleans Packet, dated May 25, 1857, is for payment of two hundred dollars, "for the passage of Mr. O. T. Morgan and Family (4 Passages) . . . from Wilton Landing to Louisville, on the Steamboat *Eclipse*—on Trip No. 5 (June 6th), Stateroom(s) No(s). 6 & 8, Berth: Both." A further note, handwritten, says "If children, Servants or Others to be paid for on board."

Also a lengthy bill of household goods, bought of Henderson and Caines, New Orleans, January 9, 1861, to be sent to Point Worthington, Mississippi. The company was located at 400 Canal Street, opposite Exchange place; they advertised themselves as "Importers of Earthen Ware, China, Glass, Silver Ware, Britannia and Japan Ware, Lamps, Fine Table Cutlery, Etc., Etc." On the bill are many items, everything from "2 doz. gilt china dinner plates . . . $4.00 . . .$8.00" to dessert dishes, soup tureens, tea sets, champagne glasses, "1 set rich Japanned waiters and baskets," numerous pairs of candlesticks, "1 rich castor," "1 blue china chamber set and 1 buff china chamber set," celery stands and fire irons and "1 wire nursery fender"—in all, several hundred separate pieces of goods. The bill comes to something over $389. Worthington Landing was chosen probably because of the constantly changing river conditions. Often it was possible to land at one spot when another, even a few miles distant, was facing disaster due to the annual spring rise. The items on the above bill, in any case, were destined for Mount Holly.

142

Appendix

Another bill:

No. 6 Higgins Block, Main Street
Bought of Thompson and Van Dalsem,
Lexington, Kentucky, February 12th, 1852
by Mrs. James Erwing [sic]
May 24 (!) 1 Crumb Cloth $9.00
Receipted Payment:
Thompson and Van Dalsem

The above company listed itself as "Dealers in Carpets, Oil Cloths, Wallpaper, Pianos, Curtains, Cornices, Window Shades, Lamps, Waiters, and House Furnishing Goods in General."

In mid-1958 I found on the back of a scrap of musical notepaper the following note:

Philadelphia 1937
In the collection of ME letters also [letters from]
Eleanor Ewing (?) (who she?)
(cousin?)
S. Sloan
? Sloan
Carrie Wilson
James Erwin
Jane Beekman
and 8 or 9 others

Had I noted or copied these letters this book would surely have been more comprehensive. It would be tantalizing to find out how these letters (some there with seeming logic, yet others utterly disassociated with the building of Mount Holly) came to be in the Rosenbach collection and all gathered in the same box. Someone was evidently interested in MJE as a personality to go to considerable effort to round up from all possible sources what was there. Still more intriguing than the names listed above is the identity of the "8 or 9 others." These in themselves, if known, might clear some of the remaining fog.

Sources Consulted

BOOKS

Basset, Margaret. *Profiles and Portraits of American Presidents and Their Wives*. Freeport, M.: Bond-Wheelwright Co., 1969.

Berkey, Andrew S., and James P. Shenton. *The Historian's History of the United States*. New York: Putnam, 1966.

Boorstin, Daniel J. *The Americans*. Vol. II. New York: Random House, 1964.

Bradford, Ned. *Battles and Leaders of the Civil War*. New York: Appleton, Century, Crofts, 1956.

Carruth, Gorton. *Encyclopedia of American Facts*. New York: Crowell, 1966.

Carter, Hodding. *Man and the River: The Mississippi*. New York: Rand-McNally, 1970.

———. *Where Main Street Meets the River*. New York: Farrar Rinehart, 1942.

Christ-Janer, Albert. *George Caleb Bingham*. New York: Dodd, Mead & Co., 1940.

Claiborne, John F. H. *History of Mississippi*. Jackson, Miss.: Jackson Press, 1880.

———. *Mississippi as a Province, Territory and State*. Jackson, Miss.: Jackson Press, 1880.

Cohn, David. *God Shakes Creation*. New York: Harper, 1935.

Colton, Calvin, ed. *The Private Correspondence of Henry Clay 1777–1852*. New York: A. S. Barnes, 1856.

Commager, Henry Steele, ed. *Documents of American History*, Vol. I. New York: Appleton, Century, Crofts, 1968.

Crocker, Mary Wallace. *Historic Architecture in Mississippi*. Oxford, Miss.: University of Mississippi Press, 1973.

Dowdey, Clifford. *The Great Plantation*. New York: Bonanza, 1957.

Federal Writers' Project. *Kentucky*. New York: Hastings House, 1939.

———. *Louisiana*. New York: Hastings House, 1939.

———. *Mississippi*. New York: Hastings House, 1939

———. *Pennsylvania*. New York: Oxford University Press, 1940.

———. *Tennessee*. New York: Viking, 1939.

———. *Virginia*. New York: Oxford University Press, 1940.

Filson Club. *The Clay Family*. Publication No. 14. Kentucky: N.p., 1899.

———. *The Johnson Family*. Volume III. Kentucky: N.p., 1929.

Freedley, George, and John D. Reeves. *History of the Theater*. New York: Crown, 1941.

Furnas, J. C. *The Americans*. New York: Putnam, 1969.

———. *Goodbye to Uncle Tom*. New York: Sloane, 1956.

Hamlin, Talbot. *Greek Revival Architecture in America*. New York: Oxford University Press, 1949.

Hughes, Glenn. *Story of the Theater*. New York: Samuel French, 1944.

Jahns, Patricia. *The Violent Years*. New York: Hastings House, 1962.

Johnson, H. Earle. *First Performances in America*. Detroit, Michigan: College Music Society, 1979.

Kane, Harnett T. *Bride of Fortune*. New York: Doubleday, 1948.

———. *Gentlemen, Swords and Pistols*. New York: Morrow, 1951.

———. *Plantation Parade*. New York: Morrow, 1945.

Keating, Bern. *A History of Washington County, Mississippi*. Greenville, Miss.: Junior Auxilliary, 1976.

Klamkin, Marian. *The Return of Lafayette, 1824–1825*. New York: Scribner's, 1976.

Lancaster, Clay. *Antebellum Houses of the Bluegrass*. Lexington: University Press of Kentucky, 1961.

Long, E. B. *The Civil War, Day by Day*. New York: Doubleday, 1971.

Longford, Elizabeth. *Queen Victoria*. New York: Harper & Row, 1964.

Lorant, Stefan. *The Glorious Burden*. New York: Harper & Row, 1968.

Sources Consulted

Machiavelli, Niccolo. *The Prince*. London, England: Bohn, 1847.

———. *History of Florence*. London, England: Bohn, 1847.

Martineau, Harriet. *Retrospect of Western Travel*. New York: Harper, 1838.

Maxwell, William. *Ancestors*. New York: Knopf, 1971.

McCain, William D., and Charlotte Capers, eds. *Memoirs of William Tillinghast Ireys*. Jackson, Miss.: Mississippi Historical Society, 1954.

McMeekin, I. M. *Louisville*. New York: Julian Messner, 1946.

McNeily, John S. *Climax and Collapse of Reconstruction in Mississippi*. Jackson, Miss.: Mississippi Historical Society, 1887.

———. *The Ku Klux Klan in Mississippi*. Jackson, Miss.: Mississippi Historical Society, 1915.

———. *War and Reconstruction in Mississippi*. Jackson, Miss.: Mississippi Historical Society, 1870.

de Montaigne, Michel. *Essays*. New York: Walter J. Black, Inc., 1943.

Moore, Edith Wyatt. *Natchez Under-the-Hill*. Natchez, Miss.: Southern Historical Publications, 1958.

Morison, Samuel Eliot, and Henry Steele Commager. *The Growth of the American Republic*. New York: Oxford University Press, 1942.

Morris, Willie. *Yazoo*. New York: Harper Magazine Press, 1971.

Oliver, N. N. *Natchez*. New York: Hastings House, 1940.

———. *The Gulf Coast*. New York: Hastings House, 1941.

Percy, William Alexander. *Lanterns on the Levee*. New York: Knopf, 1941.

Sandburg, Carl. *Abraham Lincoln*. Pleasantville, N.Y.: Reader's Digest, Inc., 1970.

Saxon, Lyle. *Fabulous New Orleans*. New Orleans: R. L. Crager, 1928.

———. *Old Louisiana*. New York: Century, 1929.

Simpson, Elizabeth M. *Bluegrass Houses and Their Traditions*. Kentucky: Transylvania Press, 1932.

Stewart, George R. *Names on the Land*. Boston: Houghton Mifflin, 1958.

Strong, George Templeton. *Diaries*. New York: Macmillan, 1952.

Taylor, Tim. *The Book of Presidents*. New York: Arno Press, 1972.

de Tocqueville, Alexis. *Democracy in America*. New York: Vintage edition, 1954.

Townsend, William H. *Lincoln and the Bluegrass Country*. Lexington: University Press of Kentucky, 1955.

Trollope, Frances. *Domestic Manners of the Americans*. London: N.p., 1832.

Vaux, Calvert. *Catalogue of Cottages & Villas*. New York: Harper, 1864.

Wayman, N. L. *Life on the River*. New York: Crown, 1971.

Woodham-Smith, Cecil. *Queen Victoria*. New York: Knopf, 1972.

Woodward, W. E. *A New American History*. Garden City, N.Y.: Garden City Press, 1933.

UNPUBLISHED WORKS

Edmonds, James E. "Lake Washington." 1899.

Johnson, Tom L. Genealogy of the Johnson Family.

White, Alice Pemble. "The Plantation Experience of Joseph and Lavinia Erwin, 1807–1836." M.A. thesis, Louisiana State University, 1933.

PAPERS

Perkins Library, Duke University
    Letters of Henry Clay to James Erwin
    Letters of James Erwin to Henry Clay
Henry E. Huntington Library, San Marino, California
    Haller Nutt–Samuel Sloan letters, 1857–1861
Library of Congress, Washington, D.C.
    Papers of John C. Calhoun
    Papers of John C. Crittenden
    Papers of Richard Mentor Johnson
    Papers of Daniel Webster
    Papers of Mary Todd Lincoln

PERSONAL INTERVIEWS WITH OR RECOLLECTIONS RELATED BY:

Mrs. Huger Foote, Sr.
Mrs. Johnson Erwin
Miss Willa Johnson
William Alexander Percy

Sources Consulted

John Seymour McNeily, Sr.
Maxwell Perkins

LETTERS TO THE AUTHOR

from

Mrs. Jessie Lucretia Erwin Anderson, 1965–1979
Mr. Wirt Amistead Cate, 1979
Colonel Robert Clay, 1976–1977
General J. E. Edmonds, 1970–1971
Mrs. Agnes Marshall Ward Gardiner, 1965–1979
Mrs. Mary Bell Miller, 1958–1959
Mrs. Emily B. Pirtle, 1929–1930
Mrs. Isabelle Ward Pollard, 1958–1972
Mrs. Ernestine Sullivan, 1976–1977
Mrs. Frances H. Wright, 1960–1979

SPECIAL DOCUMENTS PROPERTY OF THE AUTHOR

Copy of Henry Johnson's Last Will and Testament
Copy of Anne Clay Erwin's Last Will and Testament
Copy of Margaret Erwin's Last Will and Testament
Deed and bill of sale by Henry Johnson to Margaret Johnson Erwin
Land Sale of Arkansas property to James Erwin per (unknown)
    (During administration of Martin van Buren)
Abstract of title: Ward Plantations
                    Mount Holly Plantation
Biography of James Patton (autograph MS), 1756
Papers of Mary Berkeley Finke re: John Patton Erwin
                    Hon. Thomas Lanier Williams

Index

Index

Index

Mississippi River, floods of, 36, 73, 78–79, 93, 135
Morgan, John Hunt, 121
Morse, Samuel, 28
Mount Holly (house): purchase of plantation, 25, 73, 75, 77, 83, 91, 128; grounds of, 69, 79, 81, 83, 85, 90, 91, 96, 98, 113, 114, 129; plans for, 50, 53, 54, 55, 58, 71, 72, 74, 77, 79, 81, 82, 83, 84, 85, 86, 87, 89, 91; construction of, 81, 87–91 *passim*; interior of, 88, 90, 92, 94, 95, 96, 103, 104, 113, 114, 122, 137, 137n; later owners of, xvii, 136; mentioned, xiii, xv, xviii, xix, 24, 46, 47, 66, 73, 75, 101, 109, 116, 123, 126, 131, 132, 135, 137, 138
Music, 23, 27, 34, 45, 101–102, 118

Nettie (slave of Margaret Erwin), 23, 69, 97, 98, 99, 115
New Hope (plantation), xix
New Orleans, 22, 23, 27, 35, 45, 51, 73, 101–102, 105, 117, 118
Nutt, Dr. Haller, xv, 54, 94, 96, 101, 102, 103, 104, 108–109, 110–11, 112, 113, 116, 117. *See also* Longwood; Sloan, Samuel

Olmstead, Frederick Law, 72, 82

Patti, Adelina, 76
Patton, Jane, 16
Peach Blossom (plantation), 15
Pemberton, J. C., xiv
Percy, William Alexander, 101
Poe, Edgar Allan, 27
Politics, 30, 31, 34–35, 48, 50, 51, 85, 92, 93, 97, 102, 103, 114, 115
Polk, Franklin, 66
Pontalba, Baroness de, 47, 51, 66
Pope, John, xiv, 8, 129–30, 137n
Port Gibson, Battle of, 133
Pushkin, Alexander, 37

Rachel (French actress), 45
Randolph, John, 77

Redd, Thomas, 75, 96, 104, 107
"Rochester rappings," 52

St. John's Chapel (Lake Washington, Miss.), 84–85, 88, 88n, 95, 99, 100. *See also* Sloan, Samuel
St. Louis (plantation), 15
Scribe, Augustin Eugène, 45
Secession, 107, 113
Shady Grove (plantation), 15
Sherman, Eleanor Ewing, 22, 32
Sherman, William Tecumseh, 22, 26, 32, 33, 34, 49, 61, 66, 67, 77, 98–99, 100, 113, 114, 124, 125, 126
Slavery, xiv, 60, 61, 97, 102, 108, 112, 129
Sloan, Samuel, xi, xv, xvi, 22, 24, 28, 34, 35, 40, 44, 49, 54, 54n, 55, 72, 76, 77, 79, 82, 83, 84, 85, 86, 87, 88, 89, 93, 94, 96–97, 101, 102, 103, 108–109, 110–11, 112, 116, 119. *See also* Longwood, Mount Holly, St. John's Chapel
Stanford, Mary, 135
Steamboat disasters, 25–26, 28, 70
Stowe, Harriet Beecher, 51, 58, 60, 69, 87, 93, 95, 97, 102
Strickland, William, xv, 24, 72, 81, 87
Strong, George Templeton, 33, 109–110
Swan Lake, xviii

Thackeray, William Makepeace, 70
Turnbull, Maria, 66
Typhoid, 134

Vaux, Calvert, 72, 81, 82, 85, 86
Vicksburg Campaign, 132, 133
Victoria, Queen of England, 29, 40–41, 44

Ward, Emily Flournoy, 7
Ward Hall (house), 78, 78n, 115
Ward, Junius, xvii, xviii, 7, 78, 79, 80, 101, 114, 115, 122, 137n
Ward, Matilda Viley, 7
Ward, Robert, 7, 8, 28, 28n, 124

Index